"Dr. Stacy has put together a brilliant map down the 'road less traveled' that every physician should be aware of whether they choose to go down it or not. Some might pursue this path right out of medical school while others will use it for a side hustle or an encore career. Still others might simply dream briefly of leaving clinical medicine after a bad week. No matter your career goals, knowing your options will allow you to be intentional in your pursuit of self-fulfillment and service to others. More options mean less burnout and better patient care, and that's a good thing for everybody involved."

JAMES M. DAHLE, MD, FACEP
Editor and Founder, The White Coat Investor, LLC

"If you're at a crossroads in your career, *50 Nonclinical Careers for Physicians: Fulfilling, Meaningful, and Lucrative Alternatives to Direct Patient Care*, is your go-to source to find out about all the options you have to still make a difference, enjoy your work, and have a great life. Don't wait a day to read this book, it could change your life."

HEATHER FORK, MD, MCC
Master Certified Coach and Founder, The Doctor's Crossing

"Having enjoyed a career that has spanned several of the sectors covered in this book, I can attest that these jobs exist, are satisfying, and capitalize on our skills as medical doctors. This comprehensive compilation of nonclinical options is required reading for any medical provider considering taking their career beyond the bedside."

JOHN WHYTE, MD, MPH
Chief Medical Officer at WebMD

"Now more than ever, physicians have a wide variety of nonclinical career choices opening up in a broad range of industries. In fact, our firm is working more and more with physician executives who are exploring advancement outside of the traditional care industry. Dr. Stacy's guide is an excellent and comprehensive resource for physicians—at any stage of their career—looking for meaningful, rewarding alternatives to clinical practice."

PAUL ESSELMAN
President of Cejka Search

"Where was this book while I was in training? You will find not only myriad examples of nonclinical careers but also real life examples of doctors thriving along this path. This should be required reading for medical students so that they understand how to have an impact within the hospital walls and outside of it."

NII-DAAKO DARKO, DO, MBA
Trauma surgeon and host of Docs Outside the Box podcast

50 NONCLINICAL CAREERS FOR PHYSICIANS

Fulfilling, Meaningful, and Lucrative
Alternatives to Direct Patient Care

SYLVIE STACY, MD, MPH

American Association for
PHYSICIAN
LEADERSHIP®

978-0-9848310-7-4   Paperback
978-0-9848310-8-1   eBook
Published by **American Association for Physician Leadership**®
1640 Rhode Island Avenue NW, Suite 750
Washington, DC 20036

Website: www.physicianleaders.org

AAPL books are available at special quantity discounts to use as premiums and sales promotions, or for use in corporate training programs. For more information, please write to Special Sales at journal@physicianleaders.org

This publication is designed to provide general information and is sold with the understanding that neither the author nor the publisher is engaged in rendering legal, accounting, ethical, or clinical advice. If legal or other expert advice is required, the services of a competent professional person should be sought.

13   8 7 6 5 4 3 2 1

Copyedited, typeset, indexed, and printed in the United States of America

PUBLISHER
Nancy Collins

EDITORIAL ASSISTANT
Jennifer Weiss

DESIGN & LAYOUT
Carter Publishing Studio

COPYEDITOR
Elizabeth Durand

There are risks and costs to action. But they are far less than the long-range risks and costs of comfortable inaction.
—John F. Kennedy

Table of Contents

Acknowledgments

I am grateful for all the physicians who inspired me to write this book—those who asked for career advice, those who said they felt unfulfilled, and those who shared their unique career paths with me.

My sincere thanks to Dr. Peter Angood, Nancy Collins, and everyone at the American Association for Physician Leadership® who invested time and effort in moving this book from manuscript to publication.

To the book's interviewees (who are also colleagues, mentors, and friends): Thank you for the informative, rich interviews and your willingness to pass along your experiences and wisdom.

I appreciate all the readers of my blog, *Look for Zebras*, whose questions and feedback were sources of ideas on what to include and how to structure the career profiles that are included.

Scott, when I first mentioned that I wanted to write this book, thank you for replying, "That sounds like a good idea, babe."

About the Author

Sylvie Stacy received her MD from the University of Massachusetts Medical School and completed a residency in preventive medicine at Johns Hopkins, obtaining an MPH along the way. She has held nonclinical jobs in medical writing, medical education, utilization management, and clinical documentation improvement.

Realizing a mismatch between countless nonclinical opportunities for physicians and the large percentage of unfulfilled physicians who aren't aware of these possibilities or how to go about making a transition in their careers, she set out to inform and educate her peers.

Her blog and online community, *Look for Zebras*, aims to equip medical professionals with the information and knowledge needed to take charge of their professional fulfillment and earn income doing work they enjoy. It offers a job board, answers to reader-submitted questions about nonclinical careers, resource downloads, and a weekly digest of nonclinical, telecommuting, and unique job openings and consulting opportunities for physicians.

She lives in Birmingham, Alabama with her best-ever husband, Scott.

For more of Sylvie's writing or to be in touch, visit: LookforZebras.com

Foreword

At our essential core, we all want to feel safe, be healthy, stay happy, and be able to live our lives with ease and minimal discomfort. The paths we individually choose for professional satisfaction factors heavily into how successful we become in meeting those four core needs over the course of a career trajectory. Health care's frontline workforce is widely recognized as altruistic and highly committed to providing care for others; however, it is constrained and increasingly requires closer consideration for how to maintain its own wellness. Paying attention to new developments in the science of medicine, as well as those developments occurring peripheral to the core of medical research and clinical care, is challenging physicians in a constellation of ways that are unprecedented.

As an industry, health care is inherently complex. And it is an industry requiring ongoing refinements at so many levels. Arguably, health care essentially remains as a free-market economy in the United States. Assuming that premise for the moment, there are roughly 16 to 18 different sectors in the industry (including governmental agencies), each vying for their portion of the $3.5 trillion spent annually on health care in this country. For an industry that has self-recognized, it still has 25% to 30% waste and inefficiency, as well as a 10% major error rate. There is clearly much that remains to be accomplished before health care can honestly say it will be able to consistently deliver on better quality, safety, efficiency, and value for our patients and their families.

Morale in the health care workforce currently is under duress, due secondarily to increasing pressures from a variety of factors, such as increased productivity pressures, encroachment of the electronic health record, decreasing reimbursements for care, and residual debt load from training. The various environments where patient care is delivered are slowly changing as they try to expedite an improved quality of life for their health care workforces. Nonetheless, today's health care providers also must pay attention to the same sets of issues they try to assist their patients with daily. Physicians must proactively make changes to their professional and personal lives in order to remain healthier themselves.

Choosing what career path to follow over the duration of a professional life is one of the highest priority areas where physicians can truly make a significant difference for themselves and for their families.

Regardless of career stage, many physicians will at some point consider alternative career paths distinctly different from traditional patient care. Why these considerations arise is an open question, but, given the complexity of modern health care and the arduous lifestyle for physicians on the frontline of care delivery, it is not surprising.

Fortunately, Dr. Sylvie Stacy has written this book. It is an excellent and well-written resource that profiles the constellation of professional jobs within the multiple sectors of our industry where physicians can use their knowledge and experience to impact the health of individuals and populations outside of traditional clinical practice.

As we all recognize, medical school and specialty training do not provide adequate insights regarding alternative career paths—nor should they. Our training programs are rightfully focused on how best to graduate qualified, successful trainees dedicated to providing optimal patient care. Outside of those traditional training limitations, physicians must seek additional resources when considering how and where to identify alternative career paths—and this book is one of only a few select resources on the topic.

What sets this book apart from any other resources is that it is designed to be as comprehensive as is reasonably possible in a single, digestible format. The layout of the book and its chapter design provide focus on the constellation of readily attainable, full-time positions for all types of physicians. This is not a book of theoretical opportunity, but one of practical reality for today's health care market. It is a must read for those trying to answer their personal question of whether to seek an alternative career path beyond bedside care.

A favorite statement of mine is that, at some level, all physicians are leaders. I make this statement because our profession continues to be highly trusted and favorably viewed as a leadership profession. When physicians enter nontraditional work environments, the same phenomenon occurs—physicians are warmly regarded, and hopes are decidedly strong for them to create significant positive influence for those environments.

The association I am privileged to lead—the American Association for Physician Leadership—maximizes the potential of physician leadership to create significant personal and organizational transformation. In this role, I routinely encourage each of us to continue seeking deeper levels of professional development and to appreciate better how we can each generate positive influence at all levels. As physician leaders (since each of us is one), let us get more engaged, stay engaged, and help others to become engaged with creating a broader level of positive change in health care. The sphere of influence for physicians is clearly within reach and our patients will ultimately appreciate the eventual outcome.

Enjoy this book and learning of the opportunities outlined within its pages. Most importantly, continue to pursue a life where you are able to feel safe, be healthy, stay happy, and live with ease and minimal discomfort. Your career choices make a difference!

Peter Angood, MD, FACS(C), FACS, MCCM, FAAPL(Hon)

Preface

I realized early in medical school that a conventional career in medicine wasn't right for me. I eliminated medical specialties as career options as fast as I rotated through them. My future seemed grim.

I explored avenues that might leave me feeling more content than a day in the clinic or on the wards. Many physicians agreed to meet with me. They told me about their atypical careers, which motivated me through medical school.

Then, during residency, I began experiencing some of these career paths firsthand. I completed rotations with a managed care organization, a global pharmaceutical company, a professional research firm, and the U.S. Food and Drug Administration. I also engaged in medical writing and electronic health record (EHR) implementation work on the side.

I had feared that I would need to pick something just tolerable amidst a selection of unsuitable jobs. But each of these experiences was rewarding. In fact, more opportunities excited me than I could reasonably pursue in a single career. I welcomed the challenge of having to choose between several areas of genuine interest.

Nonclinical work has continued to be satisfying and challenging since I completed training.

THIS BOOK'S PURPOSE

No one has told me that I'm wasting my training, betraying my profession, or doing patients a disservice. I've been pleasantly surprised by this. My response to "What do you do?" is met with genuine interest and an appreciation of the impact of my work.

This shouldn't surprise me. But it does. Doctors with nonclinical careers shouldn't feel the need to justify their decisions to anyone but themselves. But they do. An in-depth view of the nontraditional ways in which we can use our medical degrees is simply not a part of our training. There is a dearth of accessible, useful information on the topic of nonclinical career options.

My goals when I set out to write this book were to do the following for readers:

1. To arm them with knowledge about a breadth of nonclinical career possibilities;
2. To assure them that their experience and skills are relevant to many nonclinical jobs;
3. To prepare them to take the next step in pursuing a nonclinical job; and
4. To prevent them from feeling as though they are floundering in their careers.

There is no single list of standards that define success for a physician's professional life. This book aims to support you in defining success for yourself.

THIS BOOK IS FOR ANY DOCTOR SEEKING FULFILLMENT

Medical students and residents who are—as I was—exploring the many career possibilities available to physicians—this book is for you. It's never too early to learn about where your training can take you.

Early-career physicians striving to identify your optimal path—this book is for you. The 50 nonclinical careers profiled here are food for thought, whether you're exploring the possibility of a nonclinical career or have already made a decision to transition your career.

Mid- and late-career physicians seeking a change—this book is for you. Dissatisfaction, boredom, or aggravation with your current job might spur your desire for a career change. Or you might desire to broaden the impact of your work. Regardless of the rationale for considering nonclinical medicine, making well-informed, deliberate decisions will serve you well.

There has never been a better time for physicians to take their expertise beyond the bedside. There are opportunities for all interests, backgrounds, and specialties.

Introduction

A CASE FOR THE NONCLINICAL CAREER

Our profession, as physicians, is medicine. This holds true regardless of career path or job title.

The knowledge earned through medical training is ours to keep. Barring significant brain injury or dementia, our medical experience will always shape our thinking and decision-making. It can be influential and even critical to jobs outside of traditional patient care settings.

Medical care provided to patients is informed by many external factors, such as the availability of treatment and technology, the extent to which the cost of services will be covered by a payer, and even patient preconceptions about their disease. The resources dedicated to these factors are substantial. The following are only a few examples:

- Over $79 billion was spent on pharmaceutical research and development in the United States in 2018.[1]
- Venture capital investments in U.S. companies were over $130 billion in 2018 and included close to 9000 deals, with life sciences companies reaching a decade high.[2]
- The U.S. Department of Health and Human Services (HHS) operates with an annual budget of over $1 trillion.[3]

Physician involvement in each of these ultimately supports clinicians and health care facilities in delivering appropriate services at the point of care. Beyond direct patient care, it supports the services and products that promote overall health and disease prevention.

THE ROLE OF THE NONCLINICAL PHYSICIAN

Organizations hire physicians for nonclinical positions for many reasons. One physician's job may have little in common with a physician's job in another industry, company, or even division within the same company. Nonetheless, nonclinical roles share a broad goal: to improve health or reduce the disease burden of individuals or populations. Physicians in these roles accomplish this by assisting an organization in delivering high-quality, evidence-based health-related services or products to either consumers or the health care system.

WHAT IS NONCLINICAL WORK?

The term *nonclinical* refers to work that doesn't involve directly diagnosing and treating patients.

In most cases, nonclinical jobs don't require an active medical license, because the physician doesn't engage in the actual practice of medicine when carrying out the job's tasks. However, as you'll see in upcoming chapters, there are exceptions to this. Exceptions usually arise in health care services delivery settings in which nonclinical physician staff do, from time to time, get involved in making individual patient care decisions. In these cases, the requirement for a medical license has less to do with specific job responsibilities and more to do with liability.

A physician's job can combine clinical and nonclinical work. This book focuses on careers in which there tend to be opportunities for jobs that are entirely nonclinical.

A JOB VERSUS A CAREER

A job is the day-to-day work done for an employer in exchange for a paycheck. A career is the progress and actions taken over a period of time, which often involves a series of jobs or escalating responsibility. It includes professional growth, accumulation of experience, and movement toward goals. A common way to advance a career is by leaving one job for another in which there is greater responsibility, higher pay, or work that is better aligned with your professional goals.

In practice, the terms *job* and *career* often are used interchangeably. A new job builds off of previous experience and is a natural career progression.

"Career change" is used to describe a transition to a different industry or a significant alteration in job type in response to a shift in professional interests. The first nonclinical job taken by a physician who has been practicing clinically is commonly considered to be a career change.

Career paths involving nonclinical jobs vary greatly. There is not always a distinct transition from clinical to nonclinical. Some physicians begin a nonclinical career straight out of residency. Others have a single non-clinical job that makes up a small part of a predominantly clinical career.

Most importantly, there is no right or wrong way to do it.

NONCLINICAL CAREER MISCONCEPTIONS

A handful of misconceptions about nonclinical work cause many physicians to hesitate over transitioning to a nonclinical job.

Misconception #1: Nonclinical careers are for physicians who are burned out.

Nonclinical careers are for physicians whose professional interests are best aligned with nonclinical work and whose goals are most likely to be attained through nonclinical work.

Ideally, burnout or simple dissatisfaction with clinical work shouldn't be the main driver of transitioning to a nonclinical career.

Leaving a clinical job can be advantageous for some physicians experiencing burnout. But taking a proactive approach to finding a fulfilling career is much more advantageous. This entails establishing professional goals and taking time to reflect on what brings you joy. It requires acknowledging stress, discontent, or disengagement that may progress to burnout, and taking action to address these warning signs. The best action may or may not be leaving a clinical job for a nonclinical job.

Misconception #2: If physicians take nonclinical jobs, there won't be enough doctors left to care for patients.

A report from the Association of American Medical Colleges predicts a shortage of as many as 121,900 physicians by 2032.[4] However, the primary drivers of the predicted shortage are population aging and growth. Over 40% of the physician workforce is at risk for retiring over the next decade.[5] The U.S. population grew by 24% between 1987 and 2007, while the number of physicians training in the United States grew by only 8%.[6]

Of the current physician workforce of just over 900,000, 1.3% work in public administration, 0.3% work in pharmaceuticals or scientific research and development, 0.3% work in management and scientific consulting services, and 0.1% work in insurance industries.[7] Nonclinical physicians make up only a small percentage of the physician workforce. Shifts in these figures are unlikely to have a substantial impact on the availability of physicians to treat patients.

Misconception #3: Working outside of clinical medicine is "selling out."

The opportunities in nonclinical medicine are extensive. You have the ability to be selective in the nonclinical roles you accept and the companies you choose to work for. Working in a nonclinical role doesn't mean being employed by a company with ethically questionable practices. It doesn't mean taking on work responsibilities that discount your principles. And, when compared with clinical work, it infrequently results in personal financial gain.

Misconception #4: A physician needs many years of clinical experience to transition to a nonclinical job.

There certainly are a lot of nonclinical options for physicians with many years of clinical work under their belt. For some jobs, significant clinical experience is needed in order to be considered as an applicant and to successfully perform the duties of the job. But there also are many opportunities for physicians with limited clinical experience, as well as for those who are straight out of residency and even those who haven't completed a residency.

Misconception #5: Doctors owe it to society to practice clinical medicine.

This last misconception would perhaps be better labeled as a conception. The notion that physicians are indebted to society is one that many doctors have internalized. Those physicians who truly believe that they have a duty to serve society by practicing clinical medicine are not the ones considering nonclinical careers.

A more reasonable belief is that we, as capable and intelligent human beings, owe a contribution to society. *Any* contribution to society. Nearly all of us took an oath essentially stating that we'll honor the medical profession. As noted at the beginning of this introduction, our profession is always medicine—even when performing work outside of a clinical setting. Physicians with nonclinical careers can do as much good for humanity as those with purely clinical careers.

OVERVIEW OF NONCLINICAL CAREER PROFILES

The chapters that follow provide summaries of 50 nonclinical careers for physicians, grouped by industry or sector. Each chapter offers a brief overview of a career niche and the role physicians play in it. Each includes an example of the responsibilities and activities assumed by a physician for a particular job. Other relevant information, such as typical qualifications and expected compensation, also is incorporated.

It is difficult to categorize nonclinical jobs for physicians. Significant overlap exists between many job types, industry areas, and work responsibilities. Yet, there can be distinct differences between job types even within a single career area.

Some industry segments have far more jobs for physicians than others. For example, it is easier to find job openings for physicians in pharmaceutical medical affairs than in the entertainment industry. Careers that are further removed from actual medical practice simply don't rely on physicians to the extent that the health care industry does. To address this, there are separate profiles for several careers in some industries (such as pharmaceuticals), but only a single profile dedicated to others (such as entertainment).

What follows is not an exhaustive list of nonclinical career possibilities. If you're just beginning to explore career options, you should not limit yourself to jobs described here.

A WORD ABOUT JOB TYPES

This book focuses on career areas for which full-time jobs are standard. There is no shortage of nonclinical part-time and independent contracting work for physicians, although most arrangements of this type don't replace a full-time salary—at least at the get-go.

Contracting and part-time work can be appealing options for physicians wanting to continue practicing clinical medicine while doing nonclinical work on the side. Jobs of these types are available in many nonclinical career areas, especially if you're willing to get creative in your approach to job searching and networking.

Physicians can find great success in nonclinical careers as entrepreneurs. Business acumen, motivation, and a willingness to take risks are necessary. The up-front cost of entrepreneurship can be a barrier for many physicians who depend on a steady paycheck and on benefits, such as health insurance. Those who care for families or have other interests may be put off by the time requirements of entrepreneurship. These factors make full-time, employed positions the more attractive option for many physicians transitioning to nonclinical work.

Of course, there is no deadline for starting a business of your own. Gaining experience in a full-time nonclinical position is an effective way to prepare for an entrepreneurial venture.

A WORD ABOUT JOB TITLES

There is no cross-industry job title standardization. The example job titles provided in this book are just that—examples. You might come across similar positions with different names. Some titles are used by multiple industries for dissimilar positions, as well. Medical directors, in particular, are employed by pharmaceutical companies, hospitals, medical communications agencies, managed care organizations, and more. A medical director provides oversight of the medical decisions made by an organization. Aside from that, the role differs greatly between industry and business type.

Organization size also influences job titles. Small companies—especially startups—often have a bare-bones staff. This requires them to give a single job title to an employee with a wide-ranging list of responsibilities. The chief medical officer (CMO) of a biotech startup might be the only physician on staff and have entirely different responsibilities (and compensation) than the CMO at a global pharmaceutical company.

I've attempted to profile jobs that are attainable for mid- and even early-career physicians who are making an initial transition to a nonclinical career. However, even "entry level" nonclinical positions suitable for physicians tend to be at the director level. Large companies regularly have teams of medical directors that include the lower-ranking positions of associate and assistant medical director and higher-ranking positions of senior and supervisory medical director.

Don't get hung up on job titles. Focus on purpose and responsibilities.

A WORD ABOUT QUALIFICATIONS

Some skills are advantageous for any physician job, whether it's clinical or nonclinical. These include written and oral communication proficiency, problem-solving aptitude, the ability to work both individually and as part of a team, organizational skills, ease with computers and modern technologies, and a positive attitude. Given that these skills are applicable across the board, I haven't listed them with the qualifications for most individual career profiles.

Qualifications, such as years and type of experience found in job advertisements, often are flexible. Requirements for a medical license or board certification, on the other hand, rarely are. Unfortunately, many physicians without a license and certification can't realistically obtain these. Other physicians simply don't have the desire to complete a residency. Where possible, I've included job examples for each career area that don't require a license or board certification, but that still exploit a medical background.

Similarly, earning an MD or DO is not the only route to gaining a wealth of medical knowledge and clinical experience. Advanced practice nurses, physician assistants, PhDs with an interest in medicine, and those who have completed only a portion of medical school are candidates for many of the profiled nonclinical jobs that don't require a medical degree.

A WORD ABOUT COMPENSATION

Compensation is an important consideration in career selection for most professionals, and justifiably so. Physician salaries for nonclinical jobs are highly variable. Salaries depend on many factors, such as job scope, geographic location, company type and size, the candidate's qualifications, and the candidate's success in negotiating an offer.

Salary data are difficult to identify for physicians in many nonclinical jobs. There are few physicians in nonclinical roles from which detailed salary data can be generated. Additionally, nonclinical physicians often take positions that are not always filled by individuals with medical degrees, although they may still earn more than non-physicians with the same job title.

Given these obstacles, exact salary information is not included in each chapter. Rough estimates of base salary ranges are provided for the jobs profiled in each section relative to the average salary of clinical primary care physicians in the United States, which, as of 2019, is approximately $237,000 per year.[8] The ranges shouldn't be considered definitive.

The image below is an example of how these estimates are displayed in each chapter. The gray arrow represents the full range of possible salaries, while the black portion is the estimated base salary range for the nonclinical job being discussed. The vertical dotted line in the middle of the arrow signifies the average salary for a primary care physician engaged in direct patient care.

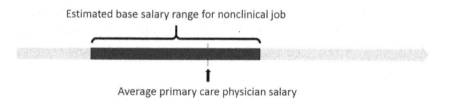

Sources for salary estimates include PayScale, Glassdoor, Salary.com, the U.S. Bureau of Labor Statistics, and personal communications.

Bonuses can be a significant percentage of overall income for some nonclinical jobs, such as those in management consulting and the financial industry.

WHERE TO BEGIN

If you're just beginning to explore the possibilities within nonclinical medicine, feel free to read this book cover to cover. Conversely, if you're interested in a particular industry or sector, you may want to start with the pertinent section.

The following list offers good places to start if you desire a certain work arrangement or responsibility.

If you want to work remotely, consider:
- Utilization management
- Medical communications

If you want to travel, consider:
- Business development, sales, and marketing
- Management consulting
- Global health
- Certification and accreditation

If you want a high income potential, consider:
- Management consulting
- Investment banking, private equity, and venture capital

If you want to work closely with other physicians, consider:
- Performance improvement and health care medical affairs
- Pharmaceutical medical affairs
- Physician recruitment and leadership consulting
- Professional associations

If you want to shape the U.S. health care system, consider:
- Medical journalism
- Health policy and politics
- Health services research

Health Care Services Delivery

Having a nonclinical job doesn't necessarily mean having a job outside of a hospital or other clinical setting. Hospitals and health care systems employ physicians in a variety of positions that don't involve direct patient care.

A select few readers may feel so disenchanted about clinical medicine that they choose to skip this section. However, most physicians interested in a nonclinical job—even those feeling burned out from patient care—may find that the diversity of organizations making up our health care delivery system offers an exciting array of job types that don't involve a heavy daily patient load or churning through a stack of medical records.

The relevance of a medical degree to most nonclinical opportunities in health care services delivery is readily apparent. This makes for a seamless transition for many physicians.

Because employers in this sector are in the business of treating patients, physicians with roles that are principally nonclinical sometimes spend a portion of their time seeing patients. In some cases, clinical involvement is purely optional. In others, the employer encourages or even requires that a percentage of time be spent on clinical duties.

Senior Hospital Administration

Growth of administrators in the hospital setting has far outpaced that of physicians in recent decades.[9,10] Although this may be a factor contributing to burnout in some doctors, it represents an abundance of opportunities for those interested in nonclinical work. Administrators influence a hospital's care delivery and services provision, support clinicians and other staff in their work, and promote and execute the hospital's mission and values.

The hospital setting is one with which we're all familiar. None of us got through medical training without spending long days and many nights on the wards. As a result, you might have a sense right off the bat whether a career as a hospital administrator is of interest to you. If you're turned off by your initial thoughts of hospital administration, keep in mind that the day-to-day operations of a hospital's patient care areas are much different than those in the hospital's administrative offices. Moreover, hospital work culture and administrator responsibilities vary tremendously based on facility size, location, ownership, and organizational culture.

As the priorities of health care systems have evolved, so have the roles of hospital administrators. Hospital leaders' responsibilities are heavily driven by a push for evidence-based medicine, new payment models, reducing readmissions and variation in care, electronic health records (EHRs), and population health.

THE ROLE OF NONCLINICAL PHYSICIANS

Most hospital executive administrative positions are not filled by physicians. Some positions, though, are almost always reserved for doctors, such as Chief Medical Officer (CMO). Others, such as chief operating officer, are sporadically filled by physicians. The exact role of a physician administrator is less important than simply ensuring that a physician's voice is present within a hospital's leadership.

Hospital administration can undoubtedly be stressful and include long hours and mentally demanding work. But these roles come with power and prestige in an organization. Physician administrators have the ability to drive significant change, improvements, and financial wins.

Employers

- Academic medical center
- Acute care or general service hospital
- Multi-hospital system or network
- Specialty hospital

The thought of working as a hospital administrator may seem daunting to physicians whose training and career have been spent in large-sized hospitals. This shouldn't be reason to dismiss hospital administration as a career, however. The CMO of a 1000-bed urban hospital, for instance, has a very different role from that of the CMO of a 300-bed rural hospital. The latter may have fewer years of leadership experience and is likely to have more involvement in the hospital's day-to-day operations.

JOB SUMMARY—CHIEF MEDICAL OFFICER

Similar Job Titles

- Chief Physician Executive
- Physician-in-Chief

Within a hospital's executive team, the CMO role is particularly well matched to physicians' backgrounds and strengths. The CMO is the hospital's medical lead, although sometimes the CMO presides over an entire network of hospitals in a single system.

The majority of the CMO's tasks aim to support the provision of high-quality, evidence-based medical care and services within the hospital.

Much of the work of hospital senior management involves prioritizing, strategizing, and delegating on projects that affect multiple hospital divisions or functions. Nonetheless, it is common for the CMO to be involved in a boots-on-the-ground fashion for a variety of situations. These might be related to a specific bad patient outcome, the care of a high-profile patient, or rifts between medical staff, to name a few. One challenge faced by a CMO is striking a balance between being involved at the staff level and effectively empowering others to take action.

In many hospital structures, medical providers report to department heads, and department heads report to the CMO. This oversight structure requires the CMO to be intimately involved in issues involving the hospital's medical practitioners. These can include matters related to medical staff credentialing, physician coordination and collaboration, educational programs, performance improvement, and addressing clinician feedback.

Cost management is an important part of the CMO role, because a large percentage of hospital costs are determined by clinical decision-making. The CMO provides leadership to the hospital's utilization management program and is involved in clinical matters related to Medicare and Medicaid requirements.

Example Responsibilities
- Coordinate clinical policies and practices
- Cultivate an environment of quality clinical care and cost containment
- Serve as a spokesperson and liaison between affiliated facilities, physicians, vendors, and stakeholders
- Function as a company-wide clinical resource
- Keep abreast of relevant standards and regulations in the managed care field
- Oversee a clinical utilization program
- Assemble and lead advisory panels and committees
- Collaborate with hospital leaders to develop and improve services

OTHER NONCLINICAL JOB OPTIONS

The traditional CMO role of providing exclusively medical administration has fallen out of favor to some degree. Instead, health care systems are hiring leaders who provide a combination of clinical, strategic, and operational oversight in a multifunctional role that is active across disciplines. They have titles such as Chief Clinical Officer, Chief Clinical Operations Officer, and Chief Integration Officer. These positions may or may not be filled by a physician.

Hospital C-suites are seeing other changes, as well. The relatively new health care executive position of Chief Experience Officer is responsible for ensuring that various aspects of the complex health delivery system meet patient needs. This represents another opportunity for physicians with interest in hospital leadership.

Many large hospital systems employ physician administrators outside of the executive leadership team. These administrators usually are junior to the CMO, and such positions provide additional options for doctors with limited experience or who would prefer to avoid the challenges of the C-suite.

QUALIFICATIONS

Strong candidates for a CMO position hold an active medical license and have completed residency.

Five to ten years of clinical experience often is expected for a senior health care administrator position. Nonetheless, when selecting a physician administrator, organizations value general skills, such as flexibility and productivity, to a greater extent than years worked in a clinical capacity.

Most CMOs are experienced leaders within a hospital or health system prior to starting their new role. Employers find this necessary to ensure the candidate has developed an effective leadership style and relevant skills. Both clinical and nonclinical leadership positions carry weight for a CMO candidate.

A master's degree in health care administration or similar degree may be preferred. Certified Physician Executive (CPE) certification from the American Association for Physician Leadership (AAPL) can demonstrate health care leadership, management, and communication skills.

CMOs and more junior physician leadership positions reporting to the CMO often have clinical oversight responsibilities, so an active license may be needed.

COMPENSATION

Compensation for C-level executives varies widely and can be substantial. Hospital CMOs earn more, on average, than clinical physicians. Other senior hospital administrators are paid salaries on par with clinical positions or higher.

Chief Medical Officer

Chief Experience Officer

2. Health Care Services Company Leadership

Health care administration extends well beyond the acute care setting. Although hospital systems may provide outpatient care in their own clinics and specialty centers, many health care facilities are independent from or loosely affiliated with hospitals.

The care provided by medical services organizations is broad, covering urgent care, outpatient surgery, and addiction treatment, to name a few. Some companies deliver services to specific populations that can benefit from targeted health care offerings, such as the economically disadvantaged, LGBTQ individuals, or the terminally ill. Nursing home and long-term care is a large segment of the health care industry and will continue to grow as a result of increasing longevity, changes in morbidity, and shifts in economic and social patterns.

The range of health care corporation services includes more than direct medical care delivery, covering services such as lab testing, blood donation, and a breadth of rehabilitation offerings.

Most organizations in this sector are for-profit. Ownership types are diverse, although many are investor-owned corporations and value innovation in terms of marketing and utilizing technologies and original ways of providing services. Some companies operate at a single location, whereas others are multistate chains of dozens or even hundreds of facilities that are responsible for the health (or some aspect of the health) of many thousands of patients.

THE ROLE OF NONCLINICAL PHYSICIANS

Privately owned organizations that operate health care facilities depend heavily on physician leadership to ensure that medical services are delivered appropriately, efficiently, and lawfully.

Employers

- Lab services organization
- Long-term care provider
- Rehabilitation provider
- Retail health clinic network
- Skilled nursing or post-acute care provider
- Substance abuse treatment provider
- Urgent care network

Nonclinical physician leadership for health care services companies often is based in a corporate office and may involve travel to facilities. Although some physicians in these roles may dedicate a portion of their time to clinical work, many leadership positions require all or almost all of the physician's time be spent on administrative activities.

JOB SUMMARY—CORPORATE MEDICAL DIRECTOR

Similar Job Titles

- Chief Medical Officer
- Director of Clinical Services

Physician leaders in health care corporations, such as the corporate medical director, have their hands in many pots. They oversee the medical aspects of the company's services at some or all locations and may directly supervise site-level providers.

Corporate medical directors work closely with operations, nursing, business development, legal, and information technology (IT) on new business, projects, and corporate-level decision-making. They also tend to be closely involved in the care provided at the company's facilities. Some are even involved with medical decision-making related to specific patients from time to time.

Multi-facility health care corporations value service centralization and standardization across locations. Consequently, corporate medical directors are involved in developing clinical policies, clinical staff hiring and training, and implementing new processes.

Depending on the niche, the government can play a substantial part in company actions as a payer and regulator. As a result, corporate medical directors are active in ensuring that facilities follow pertinent regulations. If the company's facilities are accredited, physician leadership may assist facilities in adhering to standards and preparing for audits.

Example Responsibilities

- Direct and coordinate medical management, quality improvement, and credentialing
- Provide medical leadership for cost containment and service utilization
- Review and opine on complex or controversial patient cases
- Establish goals and policies to improve the care and service to patients and clients
- Oversee the activities of staff physicians, practitioners, and other clinicians
- Evaluate trends in medical service delivery, outcomes, and practice patterns
- Represent the business at conferences, within associations, or as part of committees or boards

OTHER NONCLINICAL JOB OPTIONS

Medical leadership of small health care services companies may be restricted to a single corporate medical director or similar position; however, larger corporations and those with many facilities require additional nonclinical medical leaders working under a senior leader.

Companies offering services at multiple locations hire the majority of their clinical staff to work at a single facility. This creates a need for regional medical directors or division medical directors to assist in providing consistent services that align with the corporation's goals.

QUALIFICATIONS

Board certification and an active license are required for many medical leadership positions within medical corporations. For organizations with facilities in more than one state, multiple state licenses (or the ability to obtain them) may be a requirement.

COMPENSATION

Compensation for nonclinical physicians with health services companies competes with that of clinical work. The pay for corporate-level physician positions can be quite high but varies considerably by company size, position scope, and other factors.

Corporate Medical Director

3. Clinical Information Systems

A clinical information system is not synonymous with an EHR. It is much, much more. So, if you've been frustrated by an EHR in the past, don't let this stop you from considering a career in clinical information systems within a health care delivery setting.

A clinical information system is an organizational structure that collects, processes, stores, and distributes health information. It consists of both the technology it uses and the information it contains. By supporting tasks such as clinical documentation, provider order entry, barcode medication administration, and evidence-based decision-making, clinical information systems are an integral part of hospitals and other patient care organizations.

Clinical information systems can be specific to physician practice, nursing, laboratories, pharmacies, radiology departments, or other divisions; however, they are increasingly multidisciplinary in the hospital setting. They can be distinguished from an administrative system, which supports patient care indirectly and includes aspects such as registration, finance, human resources, risk management, and contract management. Even administrative systems, though, have become progressively intertwined with clinical information systems as we aim to use technology and processes to improve health care quality and efficiency.

Patient monitoring of vital signs, heart rhythms, and other markers through medical devices often is interfaced with clinical information systems. This permits notification of results to staff or other actions to take place, in addition to automated documentation.

Clinical information systems are complex and integrated. Their effectiveness depends largely on how they are used by medical personnel.

THE ROLE OF NONCLINICAL PHYSICIANS

The importance of physicians in implementation, development, and ongoing clinical information systems management in hospitals and health care networks is increasingly recognized by leaders in the field. Physicians in this line of work act as liaisons between medical staff, administration, and other departments to engage and guide clinicians toward optimal clinical use of information technologies and to ensure that decisions made regarding these technologies are in the best interest of both medical practitioners and patients.

It takes only minimal interaction with an EHR or other informatics tool to appreciate the value of a physician's input into the workflows, layouts, and options that are available.

Employers
- Health care services corporation
- Hospital
- Hospital system or health care network
- University medical center

JOB SUMMARY—CHIEF MEDICAL INFORMATION OFFICER

Similar Job Titles
- Chief Clinical Information Officer
- Director of Clinical and Analytic Systems
- Director of Medical Informatics
- Physician Chief Information Officer
- Physician Informaticist

The chief medical information officer (CMIO) serves as the primary physician leader for the major clinical information efforts in a health care organization. The CMIO provides thought leadership on best practices in clinical protocol development, workflows, and provider communications.

Over two-thirds of hospitals report employing a senior clinical IT leader, such as a CMIO, and the majority believe that this leader's influence is increasing over time.[11] Although the title is relatively new, many hospitals are viewing the CMIO as integral to providing high quality patient care.

A hospital's CMIO serves in a strategic position representing physician and clinician needs as they relate to health IT. The CMIO advocates and directs development and implementation of technology changes to improve care. This requires providing informatics expertise to company stakeholders, such as the board of directors, compliance officers, and quality improvement leaders. Interaction with the CMO, chief nursing officer, and chief operating officer is frequent and aims to innovate, identify trends, and address threats as they relate to use of clinical informatics within the organization.

Working directly with clinical physicians and medical staff is also a large component of the job. Adoption and effective use of clinical information systems requires training, buy-in, ongoing education, and a cycle of acquiring and implementing feedback.

It is common for CMIOs to act as liaisons to outside vendors, using clinical and health IT expertise to choose between products and develop related processes. When a hospital identifies a new health informatics need, the CMIO can expect to be intimately involved in generating requirements for an IT solution and putting that solution into place.

CMIOs must keep abreast of the clinical informatics industry direction and relate their findings back to the employer. They often participate in steering committees and task forces involving clinical informatics.

Example Responsibilities

- Liaise with medical staff to engage and guide optimal clinical use of information systems
- Provide clinical expertise to IT leadership regarding changes and improvements to the EHR
- Provide strategic and operational leadership for information systems implementation
- Lead efforts for clinical data use and develop related workflows and policies
- Serve as principal advisor to executive staff for the advancement of clinical information systems

- Promote adoption of clinical processes and solutions that involve informatics products
- Identify and pursue new ways to benefit from clinical information systems
- Participate in budget decisions related to health IT and clinical informatics

OTHER NONCLINICAL JOB OPTIONS

Physicians are suited for other positions within health care organization that have a heavy focus on clinical informatics, such as chief information officer (CIO) or chief innovation officer. Some organizations have a single position combining the CIO and CMIO roles.

As the function of physician leaders in clinical informatics becomes more clearly defined, more distinct positions may develop that are fitting for physician informaticists who work alongside or under the CMIO.

QUALIFICATIONS

A mix of clinical and informatics experience is needed for a career in clinical information systems.

Some employers place more importance on formal clinical informatics training than others. In most cases, however, informatics experience can substitute for training. In fact, many physicians who settle into careers in clinical information systems end up there following gradual, informal involvement in informatics-related initiatives within their organizations or serving on committees related to the hospital's EHR due to personal interest. An enthusiasm for technology use in patient care is essential.

A strong candidate for a CMIO or similar role has a solid understanding of clinical workflows and care pathways. Data analytics and population health strategies are likely to be a part of the position, so physicians should be comfortable working with data sets and statistics.

Numerous training programs are available in clinical informatics. Physicians can complete a fellowship that leads to eligibility for board certification in clinical informatics, which is regarded highly for CMIO positions. Certification in medical informatics, such as that offered by the

American Medical Informatics Association (AMIA) or the Healthcare Information and Management Systems Society (HIMSS), also is available.

COMPENSATION

Physicians working in senior clinical information system leadership positions receive salaries that are on par with clinical work. Salary increases for CMIOs have outpaced that of other physician executive positions.[12]

Chief Medical Information Officer

4. Health Care Quality and Patient Safety

Health care quality is the extent to which services are consistent with current knowledge and lead to improved health outcomes. Safety is a domain of quality, along with effectiveness, efficiency, equitability, timeliness, and patient-centeredness. Unfortunately, health care provided in the United States is of variable quality,[13] despite the large amount that we spend on it. As a result, inpatient and ambulatory health care organizations are increasingly open to unconventional approaches to providing services in order to improve care quality.

Risk management, which involves evaluating and working to prevent adverse events, often is grouped with quality and safety in the hospital setting. Although effectively managing risk is closely tied to improved quality, risk management also emphasizes financial loss prevention and mitigation.

With the rising importance of health care quality, independent organizations have been launched to assist hospitals in their quality management initiatives. These include nonprofit organizations offering education and other resources as well as for-profit businesses that contract with hospitals to oversee aspects of their services, such as high-risk patient care or readmissions.

Continued health care quality management sector growth is expected as hospitals adopt new health care technologies and payers tie reimbursement to quality metrics.

THE ROLE OF NONCLINICAL PHYSICIANS

Quality of care depends heavily on decisions made and actions taken by health care providers. Although quality and safety positions with hospitals are more often filled by nurses than doctors, a physician's knowledge and experience is exceptionally relevant to work in this field. A thorough understanding of challenges faced by physicians in clinical decision-making, an ability to interpret relevant data and studies, and comprehension of pathophysiology that may contribute to unwanted clinical results are all advantageous.

Employers
- Health care quality services organization or consulting firm
- Health care services corporation
- Hospital or hospital system

Some organizations have developed "clinical effectiveness" or other creatively named departments to fully capture the breadth and importance of quality efforts. With this, the need for a senior or executive-level leadership arises and may be appealing to physicians seeking nonclinical work that isn't far removed from patient care.

JOB SUMMARY—DIRECTOR OF CLINICAL QUALITY IMPROVEMENT

Similar Job Titles
- Chief Quality Officer
- Director of Quality and Patient Safety
- Patient Safety Officer
- Quality and Safety Manager

A director of clinical quality improvement or physician in a similar role provides strategic, operational, and thought leadership to support the organization's mission as it relates to quality. This individual works closely with senior leadership and department chairs to develop and implement a comprehensive quality program. Ongoing program reassessment and adjustment based on patient outcomes, regulatory changes, and shifting priorities also are within the scope of the director's role.

A quality management professional's focus ultimately is on achieving the best patient outcomes. This can be accomplished through audits, peer reviews, sentinel event analysis, and other techniques. A physician quality improvement director may or may not be directly involved in these components, depending on department size and needs.

Example Responsibilities

- Collaborate with hospital leaders to develop and implement a quality and patient safety plan
- Lead the quality department's operations, staffing, and budget
- Organize committees and initiatives to address quality and safety priorities
- Oversee measurement, reporting, and regulatory readiness as it relates to quality
- Facilitate special projects relating to quality and safety
- Establish quality measurements and tracking activities to assess outcomes
- Educate clinicians and other staff on quality and safety concepts
- Promote a culture of safety and high quality of care within the organization

OTHER NONCLINICAL JOB OPTIONS

In small hospitals, one individual may lead quality, safety, compliance, and infection control programs. The CMO may be the sole physician involved in quality-related matters. Conversely, larger organizations are more likely to employ physicians specifically for nonclinical quality and safety roles and to hire several staff in leadership positions related to quality.

A physician employed by a health care quality organization works in a consultative capacity. This work might focus on a single client hospital for months on end, or be divided among several clients simultaneously. In addition to client-facing work, responsibilities can include providing clinical input for internal projects aimed at developing new lines of business or improving services offered.

QUALIFICATIONS

Degree and licensing requirements for health care quality and safety positions are variable. What is common to requirements, though, is experience in quality management on some level. A working knowledge of the industry and associated regulations, an understanding of analytics and basic statistics, and an enthusiasm for fostering quality improvement are important.

There is no standard as to whether board certification or an active medical license are required.

Some organizations may prefer quality and patient safety leaders to have training or experience in quality improvement methodology, such as Six Sigma. Certification in Health Care Quality & Management (HCQM) or similar certification also can be valuable.

COMPENSATION

Salaries for physicians in quality and safety roles are variable, depending on the leadership level and position responsibilities. The pay for positions requiring a medical degree can be comparable to clinical work. Roles that can be filled by professionals of other backgrounds, such as nurses, often pay less. Lower pay may be acceptable to some physicians, though, as jobs in quality and safety typically are confined to regular business hours and lack many common sources of frustration found in direct patient care.

Director of Clinical Quality Improvement

5. Performance Improvement and Health Care Medical Affairs

Performance improvement and medical affairs are both focused on reaching organizational goals through competent, engaged personnel.

A health care delivery organization's medical affairs department is the "voice of the physician." It aims to support medical staff through credentialing, orientation and training, ongoing medical education, and facilitating relationships with hospital administrators. It mediates in departmental issues involving medical staff and serves as a resource regarding bylaws, rules, and regulations.

The general process of performance improvement involves measuring processes or procedures and modifying them to improve the result or increase efficiency. This includes broad modifications to organizational structure, operational processes, and employee-level efforts. Performance improvement professionals are tasked with building and maintaining a culture of continuous development that aligns with the company's goals.

Performance improvement is similar to quality improvement in that it takes a systems view of health care delivery. Whereas quality improvement emphasizes process changes to ensure patient safety and improve medical outcomes, performance improvement concentrates on human performance to achieve desired outcomes relating to organizational mission, financial management, remaining competitive in the market, work culture, and customer experience, in addition to patient outcomes.

THE ROLE OF NONCLINICAL PHYSICIANS

Without involvement from a physician or other professional with a broad-based clinical background, performance improvement efforts can culminate in a series of one-off projects rather than an ongoing program.

Employee engagement is recognized across industries as contributing to a company's performance. Physicians have an optimal background to drive medical staff engagement in a patient care setting.

Both medical affairs and performance improvement can, from time to time, involve taking disciplinary action, requesting providers to change an aspect of their practice, or otherwise offering feedback. Physicians don't always receive criticism or direction from non-physicians with open arms. A physician leader who can effectively liaise between front-line providers and hospital administration can be crucial to delivering the right messages and getting the desired responses.

Employers
- Academic medical center
- Health care management consulting firm
- Health services corporation
- Hospital or health care system

At small hospitals, physician responsibilities related to medical affairs and performance improvement usually are combined with a clinical role or the CMO role, as the medical affairs department function may be restricted to little more than provider credentialing. Performance improvement is not always distinguished from quality management efforts in small health care companies. Larger hospitals or systems with multiple facilities, on the other hand, hire physicians who are dedicated to nonclinical work in medical affairs and performance improvement.

JOB SUMMARY—DIRECTOR OF PERFORMANCE IMPROVEMENT

Similar Job Titles
- Director of Medical Affairs
- Performance Improvement Specialist
- Vice President of Medical Affairs

The Director of Performance Improvement or similar physician leader oversees projects that are both company-wide and focused on specific departments that have unique needs. Responsibilities cover an extensive range of activities aimed at ensuring medical staff success, including onboarding, compliance, and education.

Example Responsibilities

- Serve as a liaison between the medical staff and management
- Enhance physician satisfaction and alignment with organization goals
- Review and act on clinical complaints, critical incidences, and provider appeals
- Implement performance improvement processes that lead to positive and measurable impact
- Establish a process for continually monitoring and reporting performance metrics
- Supervise physician hiring, training, performance evaluation, and disciplinary action
- Create work groups to identify, deploy, and monitor performance improvement initiatives
- Apply techniques for managing organizational change and increasing employee engagement
- Identify physician educational needs and develop a continuing education program

OTHER NONCLINICAL JOB OPTIONS

Many health care companies undertake performance improvement internally, although some utilize consulting firms that offer performance improvement services. Employment with such a firm allows physicians to work with many hospitals over the course of their career in a consultative capacity.

QUALIFICATIONS

A career in medical affairs and performance improvement isn't just for the seasoned, semi-retired physician. Organizations are seeking physicians—even early-career physicians—who can improve systems and organizational structures to offer value or improve outcomes.

Successful physicians in this field are effective verbal communicators and enjoy mentoring and motivating others. Experience in data management and reporting is useful, as is the ability to identify trends and areas for improvement.

For most roles in which a medical degree is needed, it is necessary to have completed a residency and have some clinical experience.

COMPENSATION

As organization leaders whose efforts are closely tied to company performance, physician directors of performance improvement can earn salaries that are comparable to those of clinical staff physicians. Compensation for positions not requiring a medical degree is naturally less.

Director of Performance Improvement

PHYSICIAN PROFILE:

Jorge Alsip, MD, MBA

JOB TITLE: Chief Medical Information Officer (CMIO)

EMPLOYER: University of Alabama at Birmingham Health System

What does your organization do?

My organization is a large academic health center that is the centerpiece of a major health system. It is also a teaching hospital for a medical school. My department, Health Services Information Systems, provides service, support, and leadership in the use of IT to advance the organization's patient care, education, and research goals.

What is your role within the organization?

As CMIO, I serve as the clinical lead for physician and advanced practice provider adoption of the EHR and related technology. Along with the other clinically trained members of our IT staff, I serve as a bridge between clinicians and technical staff. I help clinicians understand how health care IT can be leveraged to improve services and help technical staff understand how the EHR can be used to best support clinical workflow.

In my previous role as an emergency medicine physician, I worked with a team of nurses and other health professionals to provide life-saving treatment to individual patients. Now I work with a team of nurse informaticists, pharmacy informaticists, lab informaticists, IT professionals, and clinical staff to implement technology and process changes that prevent many patients from developing life-threatening conditions.

For example, we can implement algorithms that continuously analyze clinical data and alert the care team when the patient meets the criteria for possible sepsis. By coupling this technology with treatment protocols and processes to manage patients aggressively, we can dramatically decrease the mortality from sepsis.

So, I still provide patient care in my current role. I just do it at the system level. I still work with a team to save lives. The difference now is that I don't always know the names of those whose lives are impacted.

What are your responsibilities?

I directly manage a multidisciplinary team of 25 and collaborate with a department of more than 250 staff to implement, enhance, and maintain the health care IT utilized by the health system.

As a member of the Patient Safety Committee and Quality Council, I serve the organization's leadership and patients by developing processes for enhancing clinical decision support and improving patient safety.

I provide direction for workflow optimization and process change, leading to improved compliance with state regulations, Centers for Medicare & Medicaid Services (CMS) core measures, and Joint Commission standards.

I also provide informatics support for clinical research and teach clinical informatics courses.

What does a typical day on the job look like?

My typical day starts around 7 in the morning and may include attending meetings for committees focusing on quality, patient safety, operations, or key projects, such as our opioid stewardship initiative. There are weekly departmental leadership and project management meetings.

I meet with researchers, administrators, and clinical staff to discuss informatics support for their projects. Meeting follow-up includes working with IT staff to design and test new applications or changes to existing applications.

All the while, I do my best to keep up with my email inbox, which receives between 100 and 150 daily messages on average. Just as in the emergency department, if something urgent crops up, the day's plan is set aside while I work with the staff to resolve the issue. I usually leave the office around 7 o'clock.

How does your medical background and experience contribute to your work?

Many skills I used practicing emergency medicine have helped me in my current role. As an emergency physician frequently faced with sudden patient influxes, I had to work with nurses to evaluate and manage multiple critically ill patients at the same time. As CMIO, it's vital to know how to triage and prioritize multiple high-priority projects and work with staff to come up with a plan to address them. My experience helps me to effectively tackle the multiple clinical informatics projects going on at any one time.

There is a quality referred to as "emergency calm"—the ability to remain calm, think clearly, and act quickly in a crisis. Although the number of crises we have in informatics (such as system crashes that affect patient care) is much lower than I experienced in the emergency department, that same emergency calm helps me respond to IT emergencies and work with staff to limit disruption to patient care.

What are the best parts of your job?

I've been interested in the role technology plays in health care since early in my practice. This was my initial attraction to informatics. I enjoy solving challenging problems and finding solutions that help improve the quality and safety of patient care. Over the past few years, I have spent much of my time developing methods that make it easier for clinicians to leverage technology, including applications that support the advancement of telemedicine, precision medicine, and other newer areas in medicine.

What are the main challenges you face?

Like many U.S. health care organizations, we struggle at times to meet the informatics needs of our health system with limited resources. This has been especially challenging as governmental agencies, regulatory organizations, and insurers continually increase the documentation physicians are required to include in the patient's electronic chart. As the vehicle for much of this increasing administrative burden, the EHR often is cited as a top source of physician burnout. This impedes our ability to maximize its effectiveness in supporting quality health care.

Where might your career go from here?

The short answer is retirement, since I plan to remain in this role until then. However, if I were to change careers, I would enjoy developing health care applications that facilitate physician workflow and improve patient safety.

What are some considerations for physicians interested in a career in clinical information systems?

Critical thinking skills are a must for a CMIO. Just as in traditional practice when a physician is trying to arrive at a diagnosis, in informatics we have to analyze the available information, elicit additional history, and logically rule in and rule out possible technological and workflow factors as we help investigate a potential patient safety issue. These same problem-solving skills, combined with an interest in workflow redesign, also come in handy when asked to help develop a solution for a new clinical, research, or operational need.

With the steady increase in administrative burden coming between them and their patients, busy physicians are not always accepting of change. Much of my work involves change management. Taking a patient approach is required to ensure physicians and other key stakeholders have an opportunity to develop and improve proposed changes to workflow.

Good listening skills are important to make certain you fully understand the customer's needs and any concerns they may have. The CMIO is often seen as the face of the organization's technology and can be the recipient of physician dissatisfaction and frustration with the EHR, so it helps to have a thick skin and channel that "emergency calm" I mentioned earlier.

Physicians do not need a degree in computer science or experience writing computer code to be successful in clinical informatics. There are many opportunities that do not require informatics board certification. What you do need is significant clinical experience in a practice setting using an EHR and good general knowledge of how EHR systems work.

A great way to learn about clinical informatics and to gain experience in the field is to get involved with informatics projects in your organization. I started out as the physician champion for our emergency department's EHR implementation and learned the basics of key technology, workflow redesign, and process improvement. That experience helped me land a consulting job with a major EHR vendor, which eventually led to me becoming a CMIO.

Health Care Financing and Managed Care

ealth care financing refers to the management of funds for resources needed to deliver health care. When not paying out-of-pocket, patients may have access to care by means of direct payment for services and medical products or through a third-party financing arrangement.

Health insurance in its simplest form (fee-for-service) tends to lead to health care service overconsumption. In the United States, the response to this has been systems in which medical practice is managed in order to limit high costs and overprovision of services. Such organized delivery systems are networks of hospitals, physicians, and clinics that provide a coordinated continuum of health care services to a defined population.

Health maintenance organizations (HMOs) and preferred provider organizations (PPOs) are the most common managed care organization types. Managed care organizations do what traditional health insurers do—collect premiums to pay for health care—while controlling the care that is covered. They promote member health and evidence-based, cost-effective health care through various strategies, such as utilization management.

There is a great deal of opportunity for nonclinical careers in this sector, including in the structuring and operations of health care financing systems and in determining what services are evidence-based.

Health Care Payer and Managed Care Administration

Managed health care companies aim to improve health care quality and overall population health though health care services while controlling costs. In general, they accomplish this by implementing limitations to health care provider access for members, monitoring and analyzing care delivery, and overseeing how practitioners are reimbursed for the services they offer.

Most companies offer one or more network-based managed care programs, such as HMOs and PPOs. With these structures, payers contract with physicians or hospitals that are willing to accept discounted payments in exchange for the possibility of additional patients.

Members—or patients who are subscribed to a payer's plan—have a defined set of covered services in exchange for a premium, which often is paid in part by an employer. Depending on the payer's type and size, plan members may be within a specific geographic area or nationwide.

In a shift toward proactive care, managed care companies have implemented strategies to encourage and assist members in maximizing their own health.

THE ROLE OF NONCLINICAL PHYSICIANS

Physicians are instrumental to health care payers in achieving goals. They help to ensure that the most appropriate care is being offered to members. Providing health care in a cost-effective manner is a constant challenge for health care payers. Having physicians on staff can safeguard against inferior care in favor of profit margins.

Physicians in managed care combine clinical and business judgment to provide leadership and ensure that corporate objectives are achieved. The work is patient-centered, without involving direct patient care.

Employers

- Health insurance plan provider
- Health services organization
- Managed health care company

JOB SUMMARY—MANAGED CARE MEDICAL DIRECTOR

Similar Job Titles

- Chief Medical Officer
- Vice President of Medical Affairs
- Vice President of Medical Operations

A managed care medical director is charged with providing direction and oversight of the company's clinical programs and strategies. This includes supporting clinical aspects of contracts, developing and implementing market-level strategies, participating in quality improvement operations, and heading or contributing to committees.

Medical directors may develop and revise clinical coverage policies and work with pharmacists to update drug coverage policies. This requires staying current with changes in medical evidence and clinical guidelines, as well as being able to critically review and understand clinical research methods and results.

Sales support is another key component. Medical directors participate in physician and hospital networking, market expansion, and promoting the business's services. They may partake in sales presentations, contribute to contract proposals, and work with employer groups to find clinically appropriate ways to manage costs.

One asset of physicians employed by health care payers is their relationships with other physicians in the company's market area. Whether these exist prior to employment or are developed on the job, they assist network providers in delivering evidence-based and cost-effective care.

Health insurance medical directors work closely with utilization management and case management divisions, which often include their own clinician teams that conduct medical necessity reviews. In small organizations, medical directors may be accountable for utilization management activities in addition to other responsibilities.

A managed care medical director may have a broad role or may focus on a single line of business or member population. Some medical directors manage a team of staff, which can include other administrative physicians, nurses, and support staff.

Example Responsibilities

- Provide clinical consultation and direction
- Provide education for internal staff and external providers on the needs of the populations being serviced
- Participate in efforts to continually improve member satisfaction and health outcomes
- Foster collaborative relationships with medical groups and community leaders
- Identify and implement analytical and reporting tools
- Meet with existing and prospective employer group customers to convey the company's value and services
- Evaluate clinical choices and perform retrospective claims data reviews
- Develop programs that enhance safety, adherence, and overall health

QUALIFICATIONS

A medical degree and board certification usually are required for managed care medical directors and other physicians in health care payer administration.

Experience in utilization management, population health, and quality management is beneficial.

Health care payer administration is a fitting career for the business-minded, financially savvy, data driven, and clinically focused physician. Jobs for physicians in this line of work are truly at the intersection of health care provision and business. An ability to use clinical knowledge while keeping company objectives in mind is key.

COMPENSATION

Health insurance and managed care medical directors are paid well and may be rewarded with bonus programs based on individual and company performance.

Managed Care Medical Director

7. Utilization Management

Utilization management programs evaluate the appropriateness, efficiency, and medical necessity of services provided to patients. Their goal is to manage health care costs while maximizing the likelihood of desired patient outcomes.

The term *utilization review* sometimes is used interchangeably with utilization management; however, *utilization management* is a more suitable term to refer to a continuum of activities in place to ensure appropriate and cost-efficient use of health care resources.

As with other types of insurance providers, health care payers have an obligation to compensate for loss incurred. Compensation by payers is given in the form of payment for health care services delivered to members. Without actively monitoring and managing service utilization, payers risk losing the profits that keep them in business.

Techniques used in utilization management include applying evidence-based criteria to requested services, proactively planning for medical services and discharges, monitoring and improving practitioner performance, and providing case management for high-cost cases.

Many health insurance companies contract all or a portion of utilization management tasks to independent review organizations. This practice can limit costs and encourage objectivity in decision-making.

THE ROLE OF NONCLINICAL PHYSICIANS

Physicians are imperative—and usually authoritative—participants in utilization management programs. Decisions about whether a health care service is necessary often requires a thorough understanding of disease pathophysiology, treatments, and diagnostic approaches. In complex cases, decision-making relies on clinical experience and the ability to correlate medical literature to the subtleties of a specific patient scenario.

It is not always clear what makes a service "medically necessary," even when medical literature and nationally recognized guidelines are considered. Making that determination requires that the case be thoughtfully reviewed by a professional trained at or above the level of the requesting provider.

In addition to making decisions about medical necessity for specific cases, physicians' medical expertise is needed to develop, expand, and adjust the company's coverage policies and utilization management processes. Interactions with clinical practitioners and health plan members require clinical knowledge to articulate rationale for decisions.

Whether a patient opts to receive a medical test or treatment often depends on whether it will be covered by his insurance provider. Clinically practicing physicians, understandably, can get frustrated when their professional judgment is questioned. Thus, it's critical for utilization reviews and communications to take place by someone with medical training.

Employers
- Health insurance provider
- Independent review organization
- Managed health care company

JOB SUMMARY—PHYSICIAN REVIEWER

Similar Job Titles
- Utilization Management Medical Director
- Peer Reviewer

Much of a physician reviewer's job is to determine the medical necessity of health care services, which can take on a few forms. Prospective reviews of requested services include nonemergent diagnostic tests, specialty consults, procedures, and treatments. Concurrent review takes place while a patient is hospitalized to verify the need for ongoing hospitalization and level of service. Retrospective review is performed after the service is completed and the company's obligation for payment is in question.

A physician reviewer works through a queue, consecutively evaluating cases and making a determination or recommendation for each. Although some physicians might find this tedious and boring, others will welcome the opportunity to focus on a single activity and not have to worry about management responsibilities.

Reviews are conducted mainly by chart review, although some require a discussion with the ordering provider—commonly known as a *peer-to-peer communication.*

In some organizations, a physician reviewer performs multiple review types in a variety of specialties. Others, such as large independent review organizations, hire physician reviewers of many specialties to conduct reviews within their specific areas of training.

Physician reviewers have additional duties, such as assisting nurse reviewers and case managers, updating coverage policies, and developing education for network providers.

Example Responsibilities

- Review medical charts and provide determinations about medical necessity and appropriateness
- Clearly and concisely write rationales related to determinations
- Develop and implement medical policy as it relates to health services utilization
- Contact medical providers to discuss medical necessity and rationale
- Identify patient risk factors, comorbid conditions, and adverse effects that may contribute to the appropriateness of hospitalization
- Offer medical direction to nurses and other clinicians participating in the review process
- Review appeals for denied payment of services
- Research medical literature and evidence-based medical publications

OTHER NONCLINICAL JOB OPTIONS

Large employers hire physicians for roles focusing on specialized review types or utilization management activities. For example, a medical director of appeals and grievances reviews provider or plan member complaints and appeals of denied claims in the context of company policies, clinical guidelines, and regulations. They generate final determinations and may be involved in hearings and arbitration.

QUALIFICATIONS

Insurance companies and independent review organizations seek physician reviewers with both a strong clinical background and experience with or a thorough understanding of the health care financing industry. Board certification is required, although the requirement for active licensure is variable.

COMPENSATION

Due to the need for direct patient care experience and residency training, salaries rival those offered for clinical positions. Schedules usually are limited to regular business hours, and some companies allow reviewers to work remotely.

Physician Reviewer

8. Revenue Cycle Management

A health care facility's revenue cycle includes verifying a patient's insurance eligibility, coding diagnoses and procedures, submitting claims, collecting payments, and addressing payment denials. The cycle extends from the moment the patient presents until after the patient is discharged.

Revenue integrity is a priority for hospitals, meaning that they are seeking ways to completely capture all possible reimbursement opportunities while simultaneously offering high-quality patient care that complies with applicable rules and regulations. Accomplishing this requires much more than detail-oriented coders. Hospitals dedicate substantial resources to implementing processes, software, and oversight that address opportunities for improvement in all areas of the revenue cycle.

Clinical documentation improvement (CDI) programs are a growing part of these efforts. CDI is the process of supporting and promoting accurate and complete medical documentation so that appropriate coding can be attributed.

Other initiatives to strengthen the revenue cycle include use of software to assist with coding, enhanced case management services, improvements to the denial management process, and detailed metrics reporting to administration and staff.

Revenue cycle teams work closely with quality management staff, as coding information and bills often are used for quality metrics. Some hospital-level quality data are publicly reported by Medicare and other bodies, so inaccuracies in data can negatively impact a hospital's reputation as well as its revenue.

THE ROLE OF NONCLINICAL PHYSICIANS

We've all heard, "If it's not documented, it never happened," which conveys that the hospital can't receive payment for diagnoses or services that aren't documented. This phrase oversimplifies reality, however. With the complexity of payer reimbursement requirements and coverage policies, ensuring complete and accurate documentation is a difficult.

CDI programs fail without well-defined goals, physician buy-in, an ongoing education plan, and a process that works in both theory and practice. Clinical and medical expertise are necessary to develop effective processes and to interface with clinical providers to implement those processes. Physicians working in revenue cycle management act as liaisons between clinicians and the various teams involved with coding, billing, and case management.

Employers
- Clinical documentation improvement services provider
- Hospital or health care system
- Revenue cycle contract organization

JOB SUMMARY—PHYSICIAN ADVISOR

Similar Job Titles
- Medical Director
- Physician Consultant

Physician advisors are the health care provider's voice in all activities related to revenue cycle management. They review selected health records, either concurrently with hospitalization or retrospectively. They routinely meet with CDI, case management, and health information management staff to discuss findings and their implications.

They provide ongoing education to demonstrate how documentation improvement can positively impact hospital reimbursement, practitioner and hospital profiling, and overall care. A concurrent query process may be used to address provider documentation issues, for which the physician advisor acts as a bridge between providers and CDI staff to ensure queries are responded to in a timely manner.

Physician advisors work closely with case management regarding level of care and length of stay management to proactively make adjustments and avoid payment denials. This aspect of the job is similar to the reviews performed by a utilization management medical director for a health insurance company.

The role of a physician advisor in denial management is part of a multidisciplinary process that reviews a denial, determines the appropriate response, and suggests steps to prevent similar denials in the future.

Given that certain revenue cycle improvements can be made through modifications to the hospital's EHR, physician advisors may work with the CMIO or other clinical informatics staff to implement changes.

Example Responsibilities

- Develop overall strategy to address revenue cycle issues impacted by providers
- Review patient medical records as requested by CDI specialists or other staff
- Provide feedback to clinical providers regarding documentation as it relates to thoroughness, length of stay, and level of care
- Educate practitioners on regulatory, reimbursement, and coding changes that may impact decision-making or documentation
- Identify inefficiencies within the revenue cycle and take action to resolve them
- Receive input from practitioners on matters relating to documentation or denials
- Work with an informatics team to support practitioners' ability to appropriately document diagnoses and procedures
- Act as a resource for medical staff regarding documentation requirements and best practices

OTHER NONCLINICAL JOB OPTIONS

A CDI specialist reviews charts and facilitates modifications to clinical documentation for inpatient stays or outpatient encounters to support appropriate coding and subsequent reimbursement. This individual works closely with medical coders to ensure that important clinical elements are captured when the chart is coded. CDI specialists commonly have a nursing background; however, this position can be fitting for a physician facing challenges in certification or licensure who would like to remain in a health care delivery setting.

QUALIFICATIONS

Physician advisors are expected to have a solid understanding of the challenges faced by practitioners in a hospital setting. Consequently, recent clinical experience is needed. Factors specific to the institution's CDI program and case management processes may dictate other qualifications for the role.

Quality improvement and utilization management experience are advantageous.

Certification in clinical documentation or physician advising, such as that offered by the American College of Physician Advisors (ACPA) or the Association of Clinical Documentation Improvement Specialists (ACDHIS), may be preferred.

COMPENSATION

Compensation for physician advisors tends to be lower than that for clinical work. The regular hours, predictability, and ability to work in a familiar setting neutralize this for some physicians. CDI specialists earn less than physician advisors, as most are not physicians.

Physician Advisor

Clinical Documentation Improvement Specialist

9. Population Health Management and Analytics

There is a growing need for effective disease management in health care settings and various patient populations. Hospital systems struggle to provide value-based health care. Payers are looking for more efficient and simpler techniques for managed care. CMS has begun incentivizing population health program adoption.

Population health management is an approach to improving health outcomes by aggregating data across multiple sources and using it to manage disease in a population. Incorporating analytics into a population health management tool or program optimizes the ability to describe trends, uncover gaps, and make predictions about health trajectories.

Examples of insights from health care analytics efforts include intensive case management for members with the highest risk and dedicating additional resources to surveillance for a disease associated with poor outcomes.

The word *transformation* is used regularly in this field, such as in the terms *data transformation*, *payment transformation*, and *clinical transformation*. Although it comes across as a buzzword, it effectively conveys the goal of population health management to allow for large-scale changes that will improve health outcomes and drive value in health care delivery.

U.S. health care is seeing a shift from discrete care episodes to a system of integrated care and outcomes that can be measured on a population— rather than just individual—level. This has resulted in the relatively new but rapidly expanding market for population health management and health analytics service organizations. Companies that deliver population health solutions to hospitals and payers do so by using combinations of data and science. Their offerings range from ready-to-use software to comprehensive, ongoing consulting services that includes use of both technology and manpower.

THE ROLE OF NONCLINICAL PHYSICIANS

As physicians, we're accustomed to managing a series of individual patients. Population health is concerned with the health of a group and the distribution of determinants and outcomes within that group. In essence, population health management is "treating" an entire population through processes, policies, and interventions. It requires a different perspective than direct patient care, but is a relevant use of medical training for physicians who enjoy big-picture thinking.

Subject matter expertise in both medicine and health analytics is an asset to any population health management program. A medical background allows for effective integration of health analytics efforts into clinical programs and workflows in ways that improve both the provider experience and the value of care delivered.

Health analytics roles are about more than crunching numbers. To have a successful population health management program, an organization must promote a culture that supports it and hire staff who are engaged in analytics-oriented care. The soft skills we foster as physicians are as important as analytical skills.

Employers
- Government agency
- Health care consulting firm
- Health care technology or analytics company
- Hospital or hospital system
- Managed care company

JOB SUMMARY—DIRECTOR OF POPULATION HEALTH MANAGEMENT

Similar Job Titles
- Director of Health Analytics
- Director of Population Health Strategy
- Medical Director

- Population Health Analytics Director

An organization's director of population health management is tasked with leading and supporting the population health program functions. This includes developing tools to segment clinical data aligned with population cohorts and using predictive modeling and other methods to evaluate outcomes.

The director at a health care payer organization primarily uses analytical insights to develop or improve value-based reimbursement models and wellness or prevention programming for plan members. At a hospital, the role is focused on practice models, provider incentive strategies, and disease management initiatives. In both settings, the director works to drive efficiency and integrated, shared accountability of outcomes.

Scrutinizing population health outcomes allows for iterative improvements moving forward. Physicians in this role are tasked with communicating their program's results and providing recommendations and guidance based on insights gleaned from data. Recommendations may be geared toward patient populations, providers, or both, and can involve policies or programs to drive high value in services rendered.

The impact of a population health management program reaches all corners of a health care or payer system. Consequently, this job requires working collaboratively with other divisions, including informatics and IT, quality, finance, revenue cycle management, and even marketing.

Example Responsibilities
- Drive the organization's overall population health and analytics strategy
- Recommend changes to processes and programs based on analytical insights
- Direct clinical analytics efforts to support value-based care
- Implement predictive modeling to improve stratification and population targeting
- Work with IT staff in issues related to data governance, architecture, and infrastructure
- Manage an inventory of reports and address data requests

OTHER NONCLINICAL JOB OPTIONS

Some companies provide population health management as a consulting service. In this situation, physicians interact with stakeholders at a client organization regarding their population health program. Otherwise, the role and responsibilities are similar to that of a population health management director at a managed care company or health care system. Consulting positions might have the title of clinical transformation consultant or population health advisor.

QUALIFICATIONS

Population health management is a young field that, to some extent, is being defined by organizations as they go. Roles for physicians vary drastically. Depending on the specific line of business and company needs, a medical degree and clinical experience can be required for directorships and similar positions.

Any experience with a health care company in a leadership or management position is an asset. Formal business training is rarely required, but is valuable.

A working knowledge of population health from an outcomes perspective is necessary, although this can be obtained through multiple routes. Because the field uses informatics principles, statistical analysis, and quality improvement methodologies, experience with these will strengthen an application.

COMPENSATION

Just as roles and titles vary, so does compensation. An organization specifically seeking a physician for this type of role is aware that a strong leader with a physician's skill set comes with a price tag.

Some population health management and analytics positions that don't require a medical degree are still quite fitting for physicians, although this is reflected in compensation. These may have less outward-facing or provider-facing responsibility.

As population health management becomes increasingly important to health care payer and provider strategies, there will likely be more demand for physicians with relevant experience.

Director of Population Health Management

Tina Singh, MD

JOB TITLE: Medical Director

EMPLOYER: A regional health insurance company

What does your organization do?

My organization develops and manages medical care contracts with organizations, government programs, and health care providers for our plan members. The services we provide our members include eligibility management, claims adjudication, member outreach programs, care management, and enrollment services.

What is your role within the organization?

My role as a medical director is to make sure that the provision of health care services to our membership is compliant with internal and external medical policies and standards established by the organization. The purpose of this position is to ensure we are making medically sound decisions when it comes to the services we for which we pay.

What are your responsibilities?

My main responsibilities are to review pre-service, appeals, and inpatient care requests for medical necessity. This type of work is commonly referred to as *utilization management*. I, along with the other medical directors, review requests for coverage or payment of different services. Based on the clinical information we're provided, we determine whether a given service is medically necessary. If we deem that it is medically necessary, the service will be covered by the insurance company.

A component of my job is in population health management. I assist in examining trends in various health outcomes and service delivery and then work with others in the organization to improve the metrics in a positive direction.

What does a typical day on the job look like?

I arrive to the office (or, if I am working from home, sit down to work) at around 8:30 in the morning. I spend my morning reading medical charts and requests for clinical tests and determining their medical necessity. On average, I engage in about three or four phone calls with providers who would like to discuss or appeal a denial decision that I have made in recent prior days. These conversations generally last about 5 to 15 minutes each, depending on the case complexity. I take an hour break for lunch and continue this work in the afternoon until around 5 o'clock.

How does your medical background and experience contribute to your work?

Having had training as a clinician and having experience at the bedside allows me to understand and assess requests for coverage. When a request doesn't meet a strict set of predetermined criteria, I am able to use my medical judgment to override the criteria. I am able to synthesize the clinical information and patient condition to better assess the medical necessity of a given intervention.

Because medicine is always evolving, sometimes the procedures or interventions that I review are new or different from what I remember from my time in a clinical setting. In these cases, my clinical background and understanding of evidence-based practices (and knowing what resources to use to assess effectiveness and validity of a given intervention) give me a good foundation from which to evaluate medical necessity.

What are the best parts of your job?

My coworkers, peers, and supervisor are certainly one of the aspects I enjoy about my job. They are team-oriented, intelligent, and motivated. My supervisor, the organization's CMO, fosters a dynamic that is professional, collegial, and growth-oriented, which I very much appreciate.

We have strong and palpable culture here. From the frontline staff to the leadership, it is evident that the members' health and care are our primary concerns. My coworkers' actions and the leadership's decisions reflect this value.

I love the flexibility that comes with this job. I am able to work from home and adjust my hours, if necessary, which makes it easy to balance life responsibilities (especially the unexpected ones) with work.

What are the main challenges you face?

There are instances in which my public health approach or mindset differs from that of the organization or my role. Reading hundreds of medical charts and seeing how care and coverage decisions are made for patients highlights many aspects of our health care system that are not ideal. This can be challenging, because my role is largely transactional. Opportunities to do system-wide, policy-oriented work are limited.

The other main challenge comes with having difficult conversations with members or providers who are upset with a coverage determination.

Where might your career go from here?

Thus far, I have worked in local government public health, graduate medical education, and now at a health insurance company. For the remainder of my career, I hope to continue exploring different areas of the health care system, including health care consulting, pharmaceuticals, and nonprofit community organizations. Ultimately, I am hoping to gain firsthand knowledge and experience in a variety of settings related to the health care system so I can be maximally effective in shaping health care policy later in my career.

What are some considerations for physicians interested in a career in managed care?

Attention to detail and an ability to read, digest, and implement policy changes are critical for the utilization review process.

Empathy, negotiation skills, effective and diplomatic communication, and the ability to listen and think critically on your feet are all essential for adeptly navigating conversations with practicing physicians and members who want to discuss and appeal cases that have been denied.

Typically, insurance companies like to hire utilization management physicians who have robust clinical backgrounds, because this lends itself to making sound decisions regarding medical necessity. If you are working on the population health side of the organization, an MBA, MHA, or MPH and experience or familiarity with payment models and major payers like Medicare and Medicaid also will help.

Not all insurance companies are the same with respect to how utilization management physicians' jobs are structured. In some companies, for example, there are designated utilization management physicians who work on only a single type of review, such as inpatient, outpatient, or appeals.

I recommend talking to someone at the organization you are interested in working for to find out more about what the work is like, how stimulating it is, and what the challenges are for that role to get a better understanding of what the day-to-day and overall responsibilities may look like.

Pharmaceuticals, Medical Devices, and Biotechnology

The pharmaceutical, medical device, and biotechnology industries have a major impact on both health care delivery and the overall health of the population.

A wide range of opportunity exists for physicians within pharmaceuticals and medical products. Physicians fit in everywhere from early-stage research to post-marketing surveillance, taking on both specialized positions in a single therapeutic area and broad, overarching roles.

Drug development and marketing is a complex and tightly regulated field. Certain business needs commonly are outsourced to companies that have specific expertise, reduce the pharmaceutical company's risk, or are less costly than relying on in-house teams. Contract research organizations (CROs), which provide clinical trial services, commonly are used for outsourcing. CROs and other vendors offer additional opportunity for physicians who want to break into the pharmaceutical industry or who would like to gain experience in a particular area of interest within drug development.

10. Drug Research and Development

Drug research and development involves bench science in early phases and conducting and managing clinical trials in later phases. An investigational drug must undergo rigorous testing to demonstrate its safety and efficacy before it will be approved by the Food and Drug Administration (FDA) for use in humans.

Initial steps in the drug research process are known as *discovery research*. New molecular compounds are tested to determine possible beneficial effects. Early information is gathered on pharmacokinetics, dosing, administration, and toxicities. This is followed by preclinical studies in vitro and in animals.

Three study phases are involved in clinical development once a product is approved for human testing, with each phase becoming progressively larger and more complex. Phase 1 studies use healthy volunteers to determine overall safety and appropriate dosing. This influences the design of later phase studies. Human subjects with the targeted disease or condition are used in phase 2 studies to collect data about drug efficacy and side effects. Phase 3 studies involve rigorous protocols and several thousand human volunteers with the target condition to further evaluate efficacy and monitor for adverse reactions.

It is not until phase 3 studies have demonstrated safety and efficacy that a pharmaceutical company can submit a new drug application (NDA) to the FDA for approval to market the product.

The research and development process from new molecular entity discovery through completion of phase 3 trials is a tremendous effort. It often takes more than 10 years for a drug to reach the market, with clinical trials taking up the bulk of that time. The average research and development cost for a successful new drug is estimated to be over $2.5 billion.[14]

THE ROLE OF NONCLINICAL PHYSICIANS

The main reason for the extensive time and resources dedicated to research and development is the stringent standards to which the FDA holds medications in order to protect the public's health. Pharmaceutical companies limit their risk of facing non-approval by dedicating a great deal of resources to clinical development. Medical and science professionals are essential to this process and its success.

Physicians provide a clinical voice in the drug development process to secure regulatory approvals and to confirm that new medications are both safe and effective. They do so by leading clinical development programs on various levels. Physicians in this line of work use their scientific and medical backgrounds to develop clinical strategy for an investigational drug and work with a team to design and carry out clinical trials.

Clinical trial design and execution requires strong relationships with participating clinical trial sites, medical experts in the field, and the medical and patient communities associated with the drug's therapeutic area. Physicians are key in building these relationships and using them to ensure that studies are well-designed and executed.

Most physicians in drug research and development focus on late phases of development. However, those with a love of bench research or with limited clinical experience may find a niche in discovery research and preclinical drug development.

Employers
- Contract research organization
- Pharmaceutical company

JOB SUMMARY—MEDICAL DIRECTOR OF CLINICAL RESEARCH AND DEVELOPMENT

Similar Job Titles
- Clinical Development Medical Director
- Clinical Research Medical Director
- Director of Medical Research
- Medical Director of Clinical Trials
- Research Director

Clinical research and development medical directors have multifaceted responsibilities. They interface with internal teams, external experts and investigators, and regulatory bodies. Any decisions that have significant clinical components or implications involve the medical director.

A fundamental task for medical directors is reviewing study protocols for suitability and feasibility. Directors improve a trial's chance of success by ensuring the latest scientific information is implemented into clinical development plans. They also ensure that clinical trial subjects receive the most appropriate treatment.

Phase 3 clinical trials are a big undertaking with countless logistical components. Many patient lives are affected. Medical directors form relationships with clinical investigators and provide mentoring and education. They work closely with administrators to check for compliance with laws, internal operating procedures, and standard clinical study guidelines.

Medical directors are involved in developing investigator brochures, product profiles, safety reports, and other documents. They collaborate with teams focused on preclinical studies, regulatory affairs, and medicals affairs to confirm that all efforts in the drug development cycle are coordinated.

Example Responsibilities

- Develop or review clinical trial protocols for clinical appropriateness and feasibility
- Provide oversight of medical monitors and safety personnel working on clinical trials
- Serve as a company representative at clinical advisory boards and scientific meetings
- Review and interpret clinical trial data
- Establish credibility within the medical community to carry out clinical investigations
- Interface with multiple clinical departments involved in clinical trials
- Offer clinical input for drug target identification, nonclinical studies, and preclinical investigations

OTHER NONCLINICAL JOB OPTIONS

Whereas many research and development medical directors participate in overall clinical strategy and study design, some positions are focused on implementing and carrying out a study protocol. These positions, which sometimes have the title of Medical Monitor or Clinical Monitor, are essentially project management roles for clinical studies. Tasks include staff training at trial sites, identifying process issues, performing reviews, responding to adverse events, and providing medical input for data review. These jobs can involve travel to participating sites and working closely with nurses, pharmacists, statisticians, and data managers.

QUALIFICATIONS

Given the scope of drug research and development, there are positions for physicians with and without residency training and with and without a strong clinical background. Employers may require a certain duration of clinical or industry experience. Requirements can range from just a year or two up to 10 years or more, depending on therapeutic area, management level, and responsibilities.

A PhD or extensive research experience in a relevant therapeutic area is desired for some positions.

COMPENSATION

Compensation for research and development jobs requiring a medical degree is slightly less on average than clinical work. Pay is often lower for positions in which another doctorate-level degree, such as a PhD or PharmD, is acceptable. There are opportunities for pay increases that depend on responsibilities and management level as physicians move throughout an organization or to similar roles at other pharmaceutical and contract research organizations.

Medical Director of Clinical Research and Development

11. Regulatory Affairs

Pharmaceutical companies have divisions dedicated to regulatory affairs due to the industry's tight regulatory oversight. Broadly, regulatory work involves applying governing regulations of biopharmaceuticals and devices to every stage of the product lifestyle. Professionals in this field interface between the industry and regulatory bodies. The main regulatory body in the United States is the FDA, but other agencies come into play in certain situations, and global pharmaceutical companies also must work with international regulatory bodies.

Documentation supporting the safety, efficacy, quality, and labeling are required by the FDA for approval of a drug for human trials, marketing, and new indications. Clear and concise regulatory submissions can decrease the time to move a product to market, which allows the company to market the drug exclusively for a longer period before the patent expires.

The scope of regulatory affairs spans further than regulatory submissions to include confirming that the company's actions and processes are in line with current industry practices. The field has become increasingly strategic, with other divisions relying on the expertise of regulatory professionals to make business decisions impacted by drug regulation.

THE ROLE OF NONCLINICAL PHYSICIANS

Physicians aren't as crucial to the success of regulatory affairs as they are to other pharmaceutical industry areas. Nonetheless, a strong medical background is an asset. Pharmaceutical companies seek innovative solutions relating to regulatory requirements, to the extent possible. Doctors, more so than those with basic science or writing backgrounds, can use their medical knowledge to explain concepts or present data in original ways.

The purpose of many regulatory requirements is to safeguard against dangerous and unproven drugs ending up on the market. A clinical perspective based on experience and backed by science can greatly enhance the success of regulatory submissions and maximize efficiency in regulatory processes.

Employers
- Contract research organization
- Medical communications agency
- Medical device company
- Pharmaceutical company

JOB SUMMARY—REGULATORY AFFAIRS DIRECTOR

Similar Job Titles
- Regulatory Affairs Program Lead
- Regulatory Affairs Scientist
- Regulatory Affairs Specialist

A regulatory affairs director guides the overarching regulatory strategy for the organization, as well as the strategy for each product in the company's pipeline, to ensure timely approval and commercialization. The director provides input to the drug or device development team on any activities related to regulation. The director is responsible for the regulatory activity schedule, which must align with product testing and avoid delays in submissions and approvals.

Preparing and reviewing regulatory submissions is a significant component of the job. Documents include investigational applications for new products, clinical study reports, investigator brochures, amendments and exemption applications, and safety updates. Each has specific requirements, components, and associated forms.

In addition to regulatory submissions, regulatory affairs leadership may be responsible for reviewing and approving promotional and advertising materials, training documents, and any publications that must adhere to strict regulations put in place by the FDA or other agencies.

Example Responsibilities

- Participate in meetings with the FDA and other regulatory bodies
- Ensure that trials, publications, and marketing materials meet regulatory requirements
- Prepare documents for regulatory submission and internal audit
- Respond to FDA queries
- Oversee regulatory submissions, applications, and renewals
- Manage internal regulatory document tracking systems
- Align regulatory submissions and activities with the organization's goals
- Interface with medical communications agencies or external regulatory writers
- Maintain knowledge of current regulations and stay abreast of changes

OTHER NONCLINICAL JOB OPTIONS

There are positions within regulatory affairs that don't require a medical degree but that may appeal to physicians. A regulatory writer, for example, is tasked with effectively communicating technical information to regulatory authorities and clients.

Regulatory document development often is outsourced to medical communications agencies, which is another employment option for physicians interested in regulatory science.

QUALIFICATIONS

Although most professionals working in regulatory science are not physicians, an MD or other doctoral-level degree in a scientific discipline often is required for administrative roles, such as director positions.

For positions that don't require a medical degree, medical training and experience often can replace some or all of the requirement for industry experience.

Regulatory affairs and regulatory writing positions are a good fit for physicians who are organized, like to play by the rules, and don't mind spending a portion of their time on dry, somewhat tedious work.

COMPENSATION

Director-level salaries in regulatory affairs are somewhat lower than those for clinical work. Associates, specialists, managers, writers, and other positions that don't require an extensive medical background are paid significantly less.

Regulatory Affairs Director

Regulatory Writer

12. Drug Safety and Pharmacovigilance

The benefit of a drug in a specific patient population must outweigh the risks. To accomplish this, any adverse effects found during clinical trials need to be thoroughly investigated. Ideally, a drug company identifies any adverse effects prior to approval; however, this isn't always feasible. There may also be side effects or toxicities that are known but not fully understood prior to approval. Hence, ongoing drug safety efforts are needed when a drug is being actively marketed and used to treat patients.

Pharmacovigilance is the science of detecting, monitoring, and preventing pharmaceutical adverse effects. The pharmacovigilance or drug safety division of a pharmaceutical company aims to identify hazards associated with their drugs and minimize the risks to patients. It does so through a comprehensive risk management program and by complying with the FDA's adverse event reporting requirements.

Certain drugs require more stringent safety monitoring than others once they are approved. In a subset of pharmacovigilance known as pharmacoepidemiology, adverse drug reactions in large patient populations are studied in order to mitigate ongoing risk, whether by issuing warnings, updating labels, or even pulling the drug from the market.

Some companies contract pharmacovigilance activities to a third-party company.

THE ROLE OF NONCLINICAL PHYSICIANS

Medical professionals are critical to a strong drug safety program. Identifying adverse reactions and other drug risks is not straightforward. Furthermore, assessing risk versus benefit is complex. Clinical acumen and a deep understanding of pathophysiology are advantages in almost every aspect of drug safety science.

Drug safety teams are multidisciplinary, including pharmacists, nurses, and scientists. Physicians interact with all levels of the team and hold significant responsibility for the detection and investigation of what are known as safety signals. The company gathers data about potential adverse events related to their drugs through online reporting forms, call centers, and other means. Drug safety physicians use their medical knowledge along with an array of protocols and resources to determine the best action in responding to a safety signal.

Drug safety decisions sometimes are guided by FDA requirements, such as when a risk evaluation and mitigation strategy (REMS) is required for a drug. In these cases, medical experience is beneficial in developing and adhering to this strategy.

Employers
- Contract research or drug safety organization
- Pharmaceutical company

JOB SUMMARY—PHARMACOVIGILANCE MEDICAL DIRECTOR

Similar Job Titles
- Drug Safety Adviser
- Drug Safety Physician
- Medical Director of Surveillance and Risk Management
- Pharmacoepidemiologist

Drug safety physicians typically are assigned a specific drug or therapeutic area, and play a role in all aspects of safety related to that drug or area. Much of the work involves investigating safety signals and managing the risk-benefit profile of the assigned drug. This requires working with a team to perform analyses, maintain reports, compose responses to the FDA and other health authorities, and develop risk management strategy.

The day-to-day work of reviewing cases and writing reports requires critical thinking to ensure that the information is medically sound and that proper terminology is used. Data and database review to identify safety issues requires data manipulation and analysis.

Medical directors commonly collaborate with colleagues in clinical research, regulatory affairs, and medical affairs on matters relating to risk management and safety. Senior positions often involve general pharmacovigilance team oversight and developing overall strategy, more so than simply review of and response to safety signals.

Example Responsibilities

- Lead safety surveillance activities for assigned drugs or products
- Conduct medical reviews of individual safety report cases
- Ensure that appropriate safety signal investigations are completed
- Recommend actions, such as label updates, risk mitigation activities, and prescriber communications
- Review safety report submissions for medical and clinical accuracy
- Monitor safety and adverse events in post-marketing trials in collaboration with research teams
- Maintain safety processes and systems aligning with overall business strategy and regulations

The pharmacovigilance team in small drug companies may be a part of another division, such as medical affairs. In this case, drug safety tasks may be only a portion of a medical director's responsibilities.

QUALIFICATIONS

Residency training is required for drug safety medical directors, although an active license is not needed.

Clinical experience required for pharmacovigilance jobs can vary from minimal to greater than 10 years for some senior director positions. In general, though, physicians of any training and experience level are qualified for drug safety jobs of some type.

Experience in pharmacovigilance, once obtained, matters more than prior clinical experience to advance within the field.

COMPENSATION

Drug safety physicians earn a salary that competes with that of clinical work. Significant increases are possible when moving up in seniority.

Certain drug safety positions that do not require a medical degree may be suitable for physicians, but compensation is lower.

Pharmacovigilance Medical Director

13. Pharmaceutical Medical Affairs

Medical affairs takes center stage where research and development leaves off—at the point of drug approval. *Medical affairs* is a broad term whose precise function varies from company to company. In general, it is a bridge between the company's scientific and commercial needs. It includes aspects of information dissemination, education, medical research, communications, business operations, and regulatory support.

Overarching goals of medical affairs efforts are to achieve rapid uptake of a new drug by the medical community, higher peak sales, and a longer time on the market.

A medical affairs team's activities enable a successful product launch and support the market in use of a drug. A drug launch is not a single event; rather, it is an ongoing process that aims to take full advantage of the remainder of a product's life cycle, once approved. This requires having a clearly defined product strategy, planning for competitive drug entry into the market, and demonstrating the drug's value to prescribers, patients, and payers.

The importance of medical affairs within pharmaceutical companies has been increasing. Reasons include changes to the regulatory environment, customer demand for evidence-based value, and challenges faced by drug companies in accessing prescribers and other critical decision-makers. Rising research and development costs amplify the need for drug brands to generate revenue. This is augmented by fierce competition from other companies.

THE ROLE OF NONCLINICAL PHYSICIANS

Physicians are a vital constituent of a medical affairs team. They are the medical and clinical voice of the team's varied functions. Staff with strong medical backgrounds and expertise can more fully utilize clinical data generated during research and development to drive momentum for a newly approved drug.

Physicians' experience prepares them to understand a drug's potential market impact in specific patient populations or for new indications—often beyond what was studied in clinical trials. They can assist in capturing and maintaining market share through effective education and post-marketing studies.

Medical affairs interacts with internal departments, practitioners in the disease area, payers, government bodies, academia, and consumers. These are key stakeholders in the success of a medical affairs team. Physicians can use their experience to inform the communication of scientific evidence to each group.

Employers
- Contract medical affairs organization
- Contract research organization
- Pharmaceutical company

JOB SUMMARY—MEDICAL AFFAIRS MEDICAL DIRECTOR

Similar Job Titles
- Director of Medical and Scientific Affairs
- Medical Advisor
- Medical Lead
- Scientific Affairs Medical Director

Medical affairs medical directors spend their time on activities that align science and business as they relate to the company's drug or therapeutic area. They ensure that sales and marketing strategies are based on accurate clinical data and that necessary information is disseminated to health care professionals and patients who use or may potentially use a drug.

Medical directors are involved in pharmaceutical medical education, in which programs are developed and presented to inform medical professionals about the diseases, treatments, uses, and trial data relevant to the company's products.

They assist in developing post-marketing studies, which are also known as phase 4 trials. A director might, for example, conduct scientific advisory board meetings to identify new research opportunities, provide guidance on study design, and plan for subsequent publications.

A medical affairs director may serve as a source of scientific knowledge for data review, give input on product labeling, and evaluate the language used for advertising, publications, and education.

Example Responsibilities

- Provide clinical and medical guidance to the medical affairs team
- Plan and strategize for scientific meetings and advisory boards
- Offer scientific input into publication strategy, manuscripts, and abstracts
- Contribute to the development and execution of brand strategy from a medical standpoint
- Cultivate partnerships with patient groups and relevant professional societies
- Review medical content for the company's publications and education activities
- Keep abreast of relevant scientific information through literature and conferences
- Lead cross-functioning teams in post-marketing study design and publications
- Develop internal training activities related to a therapeutic area or drug product

Many medical directors are assigned to a specific therapeutic area. Within that area, many physicians—especially those in small medical affairs teams—have a broad role. At larger companies with multiple medical directors working in a therapeutic area, each physician may have a focus area, such as consumers or global strategy.

JOB SUMMARY—MEDICAL SCIENCE LIAISON

Similar Job Titles

- Clinical Science Liaison
- Field Director

- Medical Scientist
- Regional Medical Liaison

Most medical affairs divisions have a field-based team that acts as a link between pharmaceutical companies and the medical and scientific community.

As drug development shifts toward personalized medicine, rare diseases, and specialty drugs, it is becoming increasingly important that prescribers understand clinical data, indications, and drug information.

A medical science liaison (MSL) is responsible for interfacing between the company and outside health care professionals. MSLs provide education and guidance by developing presentations and learning tools to communicate scientific data. They form relationships with thought leaders to assist in distributing information and to gain insight from the field. In doing so, strict regulations must be adhered to, such as those relating to discussion of off-label drug uses.

Example Responsibilities

- Monitor the external landscape as it relates to the company's products and therapeutic area
- Engage in scientific dialogue and build relationships with key opinion leaders
- Respond to inquiries while maintaining consistency with compliance requirements
- Deploy resources to a geographic region to support business objectives
- Disseminate scientific information within the professional community
- Work with a team of other MSLs to develop and implement a medical science strategy
- Maintain up-to-date scientific and clinical knowledge of a therapeutic area
- Identify and address needs of clinical organizations in a geographic territory
- Recognize opportunities for new projects, studies, or initiatives in a therapeutic area

QUALIFICATIONS

Requirements for medical affairs medical directors are variable across companies and even across teams within a single company, and depend on the drug type, team size, marketing strategy, and other factors.

Experience in or knowledge of the pertinent therapeutic area is important. Some positions require board certification and extensive specialty clinical experience. Others require industry experience, regardless of the therapeutic area.

Many companies place value on having field-based medical affairs teams with diverse backgrounds and experience. MSLs usually hold a PhD or PharmD degree, although it is not uncommon for MSLs to have an MD or other clinically based credential, such as NP, PA, or even RN. Some companies allow a physician candidate's clinical experience within a therapeutic area to take the place of industry experience.

COMPENSATION

Medical affairs medical directors usually are well compensated, although salaries vary considerably. Positions requiring training in a highly compensated medical specialty pay more than others.

Because a medical degree is not required for MSL positions, compensation is lower. A perk for some MSLs and a drawback for others is that time spent traveling can be extensive, depending on the geographic territory for which the MSL is responsible.

Medical affairs physicians are well-positioned to advance in both responsibility and salary.

Medical Affairs Medical Director

Medical Science Liaison

14. Health Economics, Market Access, and Managed Markets

Health economics is concerned with effectiveness, value, and behavior as it relates to health care consumption. Health economics and outcomes research (HEOR) within a pharmaceutical company aims to collect and disseminate data on a drug after approval. It tends to focus on humanistic data, such as health-related quality of life and other patient-reported outcomes. This field has grown rapidly as governments and payers grapple with how to provide the best possible health outcomes to their populations.

This field encompasses pharmacoeconomics, a discipline that compares the value of one drug or therapy with another. Health care decision-makers are faced with selecting interventions from multiple treatment options, making HEOR pivotal in achieving success during a drug's post-approval lifecycle.

HEOR often is structured as a component of medical affairs; however, it is closely associated with aspects of commercial divisions, including market access, managed markets, and marketing.

Market access is the process used to ensure that all appropriate patients have rapid and continued access to a product at the right price. Its strategy aims to identify markets for a drug and any commercial considerations that will affect how that strategy is carried out. This is traditionally accomplished by understanding needs of physicians and pharmacies and engaging with these groups.

The scope of market access has shifted in recent years from a price-based to a value-based approach. In addition to physicians, it now includes stakeholders in the commercial environment, such as patients, payers, and advocacy groups who might impact treatment decision-making.

A managed markets division functions to ensure profitable access to patients through promoting drugs' advantages. This is done through communications and contracting with managed care customers, including both commercial and federal health care payers. This differs from traditional marketing by its emphasis on the payer and, therefore, a need for different messaging.

THE ROLE OF NONCLINICAL PHYSICIANS

Due to the pivot in commercial strategy from simple product pricing toward establishing value and demonstrating health outcomes, professionals with medical backgrounds are now a significant component of HEOR, market access, and managed market teams. Success in this field requires a solid understanding of customer needs and concerns, which often are clinical in nature. They are best understood by someone who has practiced in a clinical setting.

Demonstrating a medical product's economic value is complex. As opposed to clinical trials, whose outcomes are often straightforward clinical findings, HEOR relies on patient-reported data, quality of life measurements, cost-effective analyses, and other evaluative techniques. These require assumptions and extrapolations that can lead to skewed, irrelevant results unless decisions related to methods and analyses are clinically and scientifically sound.

Recent developments in research methodologies further enhance the need for physician contributions to the field.

Employers
- Contract research organization
- HEOR consulting firm
- Pharmaceutical company

JOB SUMMARY—HEALTH ECONOMICS AND OUTCOMES RESEARCH DIRECTOR

Similar Job Titles
- HEOR Liaison
- Health Economist

- Medical Director of Economics and Outcomes

Physicians in this role interact with commercial team members as well as with clinical staff in other divisions in order to understand and communicate economic evidence to support drug marketing and pricing. Externally, physicians in HEOR are responsible for demonstrating the value of the company's drugs to health care payers.

With regard to research activities, an HEOR director oversees analyses to support marketing decisions and to assist health care providers and payers in delivering cost-effective solutions. The director is involved in all research aspects, including study design and implementation, data analysis, and results dissemination.

Product access activities may be a part of an HEOR director's role. This involves identifying and engaging with the patient community, communicating the drug's value, monitoring trends in payer organizations, and troubleshooting issues related to reimbursement.

Example Responsibilities
- Guide and perform HEOR studies
- Inform marketing, medical affairs, and sales strategies through the use of health economics data
- Work with functional departments to align market access strategy
- Ensure that product publications and materials are aligned with customer, prescriber, and payer needs
- Facilitate meetings with government agencies, policy makers, and payers
- Develop and execute plans to meet payer and provider requirements for reimbursement
- Support and sustain payer drug coverage through research and analyses
- Develop recommendations to overcome economic barriers to market adoption

OTHER NONCLINICAL JOB OPTIONS

Pharmaceutical companies often outsource health economics activities to consulting companies due to their highly analytical and technical nature. These companies represent an alternative employer for physicians in this line of work.

Some managed markets positions are field-based within a geographic territory, similar to an MSL team structure. Field-based roles are focused on forming relationships and collaborating with external stakeholders. Gathering and reporting on field insights that inform HEOR and marketing strategy is a large component of field-based jobs. External meetings and presentations are emphasized more than in corporate-based positions.

QUALIFICATIONS

Most positions in HEOR don't require a medical degree, but do require a doctorate. Some companies may see more value in a physician's clinical background for this type of role than others. Experience in various care delivery and payer settings is an asset, because this work requires a solid understanding of a range of health care environments.

Highly qualified applicants have research experience, especially in economic modeling, claims analysis, and observational studies. Statistics knowledge and an understanding of health policy, economics, and epidemiology are important.

COMPENSATION

Compensation in HEOR—even in director-level positions—is lower than in clinical work.

Physicians in HEOR positions are equipped to transfer to positions in medical affairs, research and development, and other pharmaceutical divisions.

Health Economics and Outcomes Research Director

Biotechnology Industry

Biotechnology is the use of living systems and organisms to make products for a specific use. Interferons, monoclonal antibodies, recombinant proteins, molecular diagnostics, cell and gene therapies, and vaccines are all medical applications of biotechnologies. The "technology" component of biotechnology encompasses a broad range of techniques for modifying living systems so that they can be used for medical and nonmedical purposes, including genomics, proteomics, or sequencing.

Biotechnology products have a biologic basis, as opposed to the traditional chemical basis of pharmaceutical products. Some products, however, do not fit discretely in one category or another—for instance, certain combination products and drug delivery systems. Additionally, many large pharmaceutical companies now develop and market biologically based products in addition to chemical compounds. As a result, the distinction between the biotechnology and pharmaceutical industries is blurred.

Colloquially, the term *biotech* is used to refer to small, development-stage companies that are in the midst of securing funding and are likely to be bought up by a larger organization if successful. This makes for a significantly different working environment and responsibilities for employees. For the purposes of the information here, the biotechnology industry is loosely considered to be composed of such startups.

THE ROLE OF NONCLINICAL PHYSICIANS

Biotech startups are powered largely by master's- and PhD-level scientists. A physician's skill set stands apart in that it provides insight into questions and challenges related to clinical, health care, and pathophysiologic topics.

Compared with established pharmaceutical companies, biotech startups tend to have bare-bones staffing and are driven by a short financial runway. As a result, hours can be long, and changes can happen quickly. Physicians often assume a broad role that involves input and decision-making in any area needing medical or clinical expertise.

Employers
- Medical biotechnology company
- Pharmaceutical company with biotechnology products

JOB SUMMARY—DIRECTOR OF SCIENTIFIC OPERATIONS

Similar Job Titles
- Chief Medical Officer
- Medical Director
- Vice President

Although roles and responsibilities vary greatly in young biotech companies, a medical director, CMO, or similar position usually is responsible for aspects of product development strategy execution. Clinical input is needed for study protocol development and implementation, regulatory issues, monitoring and reviewing safety information, data analysis, manuscript writing and submission, and data presentation at scientific meetings.

Many positions have a strong outward-facing presence, with the physician portraying the face of the company in order to build recognition and relationships with the health care and academic communities.

Example Responsibilities
- Oversee clinical development of biotechnology products
- Represent the company in academic and clinical settings
- Develop strategic relationships with physicians and clinical investigators
- Evaluate clinical study protocols and assist study investigators
- Organize and moderate scientific expert panels and advisory boards
- Provide analysis and review of clinical data and publications
- Assist with document preparation and submission to regulatory authorities
- Identify new opportunities for clinical development

OTHER NONCLINICAL JOB OPTIONS

Whether a biotech company has other positions suitable for physicians depends largely on its size. Larger companies may hire physicians for more specific functions than small or startup biotech companies.

QUALIFICATIONS

Positions in the biotechnology industry that require a medical degree often also require extensive industry experience and familiarity with the medical product research and development process.

For physicians with a PhD or strong research background, a research and development position that doesn't necessarily require an MD may be fitting.

COMPENSATION

Differences in requirements, responsibilities, and employers make it difficult to pinpoint an average salary. In general, base salaries offered by startup companies are lower than salaries of larger, established companies. Startups regularly offer ownership stake in the company, however, which can be quite rewarding if the company is successful.

Director of Scientific Operations

16. Medical Device Industry

Medical devices have significantly improved management of numerous disease states, reduced the invasiveness and length of surgeries, and lowered certain medical costs. Examples include insulin pumps, surgical instruments, irradiation apparatuses, laboratory systems, and various medical appliances.

This field will continue to grow. Medical devices have become progressively more sophisticated, complementary to biotechnologies, and smaller. They are expected to be increasingly involved in delivering pharmaceutical products, such as with drug-coated stents, skin patches, and specialized needles and pumps that control drug delivery. Complex materials, including bioabsorbable and nanomaterials, are being used in medical devices. There is also a shift toward marketing certain devices directly to patients.

As with pharmaceuticals, medical devices are regulated by the FDA; however, the regulations themselves are quite different. Devices are classified by their level of risk to the patient or user. Medical device clinical trials utilize fewer subjects and healthy controls.

THE ROLE OF NONCLINICAL PHYSICIANS

Physicians often are involved in the development of medical devices to a greater extent than that of pharmaceuticals. Whereas drug effects can be adequately tested in clinical trials, medical device success depends on more than its effect on patients or a particular disease state. Devices must be operated, implanted, or otherwise handled by practicing clinicians in order to have a positive impact on a patient's health. If a device is difficult to handle or poorly designed, it is unlikely to be used. As a result, a medical background is imperative in device development and marketing.

Medical knowledge and experience working in health care delivery settings gives physicians insight into clinical needs and a sense of what the feasible solutions are to problems that can be solved with medical devices.

Practicing physicians are an important source of information and knowledge related to unmet needs, preferences, and potential opportunities for new or refined medical devices. The ability of industry physicians to interface with practicing doctors is valuable.

Medical device companies face competition from imitators that enter the market quickly after a product is released. A key challenge that physicians can assist with is anticipating market demand and providing input into market strategy to encourage early adoption.

Employers
- Contract research organization
- Medical device company

JOB SUMMARY—DIRECTOR OF CLINICAL AFFAIRS

Similar Job Titles
- Medical Affairs Director
- Medical Director
- Scientific Director

The director of clinical affairs or employee with a similar role in the medical device industry acts as a strategic partner with colleagues in research and development, clinical studies, regulatory science, and marketing. The director provides medical and scientific input for each division, based on specific product needs at a given point in development or commercialization.

In most cases, clinical affairs directors strategize and collaborate with other company leaders as well as interact with external stakeholders. They must ensure that business strategy aligns with medical and scientific knowledge, ethics, regulation, and practice.

Example Responsibilities
- Serve as a clinical expert to provide insights and thought leadership across the business

- Provide clinical insight to medical affairs and commercial teams
- Oversee clinical study protocol development and implementation
- Utilize a medical background to resolve clinical development problems
- Manage FDA submissions, articles, and abstract writing
- Present at relevant scientific conferences
- Interface with external experts, investigators, and key opinion leaders

OTHER NONCLINICAL JOB OPTIONS

Jobs in the medical device industry that may be fitting for physicians with limited training or clinical experience include roles in product training, such as clinical training specialist and field training manager. These are field-based positions that work closely with clinicians to ensure a device is being used properly and to assist with rapid market uptake of new devices.

QUALIFICATIONS

Both research and clinical experience are common requirements for physicians seeking employment with medical device companies. Industry experience is necessary for some positions.

Requirements can vary considerably based on company size, device type, and whether the position is more of a generalist role or a directorship within a specific team, such as clinical development or medical affairs.

More so than in pharmaceuticals, careers in medical devices are fitting for physicians with engineering backgrounds. Although physician roles may not require actual engineering responsibilities, an understanding of biomedical engineering, mechanical engineering, or electrical engineering can be an asset.

Positions focused on product training do not require a medical degree, but do benefit from knowledge of health care delivery settings and physician practices, as well as clinical experience.

COMPENSATION

As with qualifications, compensation is variable in medical device jobs. Positions requiring an MD can be accompanied by salaries that rival clinical work. However, even medical director positions in this industry do not always require an MD. Other practitioner degrees or PhDs are sometimes accepted. In those situations, compensation can be lower.

Salaries for field-based positions, such as clinical training roles, typically do not reach six figures.

Director of Clinical Affairs

Ruth Namuyinga, MD, MPH

JOB TITLE: Director, Clinical Safety and Pharmacovigilance

EMPLOYER: A medium-sized pharmaceutical company

What does your organization do?

I work for a company that has historically developed pharmacologic therapies in the areas of cardiovascular disease and pain management. More recently, they've shifted focus to oncology. They have products in various stages of clinical development for multiple cancer types.

The Clinical Safety and Pharmacovigilance division is responsible for providing safety oversight for company products. We characterize the safety profile of drugs or compounds in development. We then determine approaches for preventing or reducing the severity of adverse events among patients. These strategies are communicated to patients and prescribing physicians.

What is your role within the organization?

I work as part of a team that characterizes the safety profile of assigned products, conducts surveillance of adverse events in the population, and develops risk minimization strategies to reduce harm in patients.

The purpose of this role is to communicate key safety information to departments to guide decisions in appropriate drug use, both in clinical trials and in the general population.

What are your responsibilities?

I provide individual medical review and assessment of reported adverse events. I perform aggregate assessments of adverse event data on a periodic basis to evaluate for signals that may point to a new safety issue or a change in occurrence of a known safety issue. I author documents, such as investigator brochures and informed consent forms, that guide investigators conducting clinical trials, as well as periodic aggregate safety reports for regulatory purposes. These are submitted to the FDA and European Medicines Agency. Aggregate safety reports are mandated by health authorities to ensure adequate safety monitoring for drugs in development or those already approved for use.

I collaborate closely with other functions and departments, such as biostatistics, medical affairs, and regulatory affairs to analyze safety data and communicate this information to patients, prescribing physicians, and regulatory agencies.

What does a typical day on the job look like?

The average day does not quite exist. Each day calls for different responsibilities, depending on what needs my attention at the moment. Typically, I start my workday at 8 in the morning with catching up on email. I attend meetings with the safety team to review new or ongoing safety concerns. Between meetings, I author reports or analyze data to support an ongoing safety investigation. My workday usually ends by 5 in the evening.

How does your medical background and experience contribute to your work?

The foundation of what I do is based on an understanding of medicine. A good understanding of the pathophysiology and epidemiology of the underlying disease as well as the safety profile of current therapies is required.

It is important to understand the biologic mechanism of the drug, because this plays into determination of potential causality. Without knowing what effects may be due to the underlying disease or concurrent treatments, it is difficult to ascertain effects associated with a new drug.

What are the best parts of your job?

It is like detective work. I never know what to make of a reported event until I dig into the data and understand it. Sometimes unexpected associations emerge that may have gone undetected. This means that each day is different.

I like the work–life balance this role allows. I don't typically work on weekends or evenings.

What are the main challenges you face?

It is often challenging to determine causality. Many patients in oncology are very sick, and some have tried multiple therapies. They get enrolled into clinical trials as a last resort. Determining which adverse events are associated with the experimental treatment in this patient population is quite challenging, because these same events may be due to concurrent therapies or the underlying malignancy.

Where might your career go from here?

I don't know where it will take me. But I hope to enhance pharmacovigilance activities in parts of the world where this is not yet as strong. Perhaps I'll partner with the World Health Organization (WHO) or another international health agency in strengthening pharmacovigilance at the global level.

What are some considerations for physicians interested in a career in drug safety?

Physicians with diverse backgrounds work in drug safety and pharmacovigilance. Having prior experience in clinical research, with the FDA, or in a different function in the pharmaceutical industry is helpful. In addition to a medical degree, training in epidemiology provides additional skills that are useful in getting the job done.

Drug safety physicians need to be flexible in taking on whatever is thrown at them. This career may not be the right fit for physicians who prefer a predicable set of tasks each day. The work requires cross-functional collaboration, so you need to be comfortable working in teams.

This is a highly regulated environment that requires reporting to the FDA and other regulatory bodies and health authorities. The work has to be in compliance with regulations set by these agencies, so keeping up with the current regulations is key.

Technology and Innovation

Biomedical innovation transcends drugs and devices. Much of this innovation builds on, borrows from, or is influenced by technological innovation in other fields. Progressively powerful hardware and software, data management capabilities, and analytics tools being used by a variety of sectors, including finance and consumer marketing, are shaping foundations for use in health care.

Digitized information is ubiquitous. It has become increasingly common for qualitative aspects of life to be converted to quantified data. Rapid growth in the use of mobile phones, for example, has led to personal sensors becoming a part of everyday life for many Americans. The result is large volumes of data being generated quickly. Health care data can be measured in petabytes. (For reference, a petabyte is one million gigabytes.)

We're faced with the challenge of how to effectively use health care innovations as a tool, rather than an impediment. Barriers to the adoption and success of technological innovation in health care include evolving regulation, privacy and security concerns, and resistance to change. Physicians are needed to provide medical expertise in technology development, identify and guide new applications, and support implementation.

17. Health Information Technology

Health IT involves the use of electronics to store, retrieve, and manipulate health-related information and data. It supports information management and exchange in any health care delivery or patient care context through software-based solutions.

Health IT is distinct from health informatics. The latter, which includes the subdisciplines of medical informatics, public health informatics, and others, uses data from health information technologies to improve health care services through organization, security, evaluation, and sharing of that data. Nonetheless, many jobs combine aspects of both disciplines.

Given the breadth of applications for health IT, the types of technology in this field are extensive. Health IT products include EHRs, software for computerized physician order entry and e-prescribing, electronic medication administration records and barcoding, quality assurance analysis software, network security solutions, telehealth integrations, and personal health records. Likewise, there is an array of organizations who hire staff in health IT roles, spanning private industry, government, and academia.

EHRs are perhaps the most widespread and valuable tool used by physicians in health IT. EHR systems have changed that way that health care is delivered in virtually every setting. They are not simply digital versions of paper charts. Instead, they are tools for improving patient care that often impact entire workflows and decision-making processes.

THE ROLE OF NONCLINICAL PHYSICIANS

In a way, physicians in the health IT industry are health care translators. They translate clinical and medical knowledge to a usable format for a health IT product. When the product is marketed, they translate its value to health care customers and providers in a way that is relatable from a clinical viewpoint.

A common complaint regarding health IT products is that they appear to have been developed without a physician's input. The value of a physician's medical knowledge and clinical experience in the decisions that go into developing a system is clear. An EHR or any other health IT product that aligns with physicians' thought processes and management approaches can offer efficiency, time savings, more useful data, and better outcomes.

Employers

- EHR or other software company
- Health IT consulting firm
- Health IT vendor

JOB SUMMARY—PHYSICIAN EXECUTIVE

Similar Job Titles

- Director of Medical Informatics
- EHR Specialist
- Physician Consultant

A health IT physician executive acts as both a medical subject matter expert and a liaison to the medical community.

With EHRs and other health IT solutions, a sales transaction is not a discrete event. Rather, the product comes with a service, often including customization, implementation, training, and ongoing support.

Physician executives partner with administration and clinicians at client or customer institutions to improve performance of and satisfaction with the company's product. They facilitate clinical discussions with clients related to adopting the technology and aligning it with their processes and objectives. This requires being able to articulate the rationale for various features and best practices for use.

Supporting the sales process is a crucial part of a physician executive's role. Potential customers, such as hospitals and medical practices, have physicians or other clinicians on the decision-making team. They have clinical questions and skepticisms that are best addressed by a peer. Some prospective clients, including those that are part of or affiliated with local, state, or federal governments, may use formal requests for proposal (RFP) processes to select a vendor for their health IT needs. Physician executives assist in this process through contributing to RFP responses, demonstrating the product, and assisting in training and deployment for successful bids.

Example Responsibilities

- Provide medical expertise for strategy and product development
- Develop relationships with business partners and current or potential customers
- Leverage the use of analytics to promote product adoption and optimization
- Work with developers to optimize a health IT product based on clinical best practices and workflows
- Identify and resolve barriers to technology use in health care settings
- Develop training programs for internal staff and customers

OTHER NONCLINICAL JOB OPTIONS

Health IT companies hire professionals with clinical backgrounds for a variety of roles. Some positions that do not require a medical degree can still be a good fit for physicians. A health care software specialist or EHR implementation specialist, for example, delivers training and assistance to health care staff during an IT go-live or when a significant product change is made. Some companies hire physicians in these roles in order to offer peer support during implementation.

Physicians with experience in software development or coding have a unique skill set. This combination opens up doors to unconventional positions and consulting opportunities within the industry.

Consumer health IT is a growing field at the junction of health IT, health education, and public health, with opportunities for physician involvement. It includes applications that are aimed at encouraging patients to take an active role in managing their health by providing tools for them to control their health information electronically, communicate with health care professionals, and make decisions about their care.

QUALIFICATIONS

An interest in technologies as they relate to health care is a must. Physicians in this field should have experience using health technologies throughout their own career. Experience using the company's own product in a clinical setting is required for certain positions.

A health IT or informatics certification, such as Certified Professional in Electronic Health Records (CPEHR), may be considered a plus, but is not generally required for physicians.

COMPENSATION

Compensation and benefits to physicians in the health IT field depend on many elements related to both the company and the physician's responsibility level.

Physician Executive

Implementation Specialist

18. Artificial Intelligence and Machine Learning

"Every aspect of learning or any other feature of intelligence can be so precisely described that a machine can be made to simulate it." This statement, which was printed on the proposal for a Dartmouth-sponsored artificial intelligence workshop when the field was in its infancy in the 1950s, is not something that most physicians want to hear. It conjures thoughts of being replaceable and unnecessary. Until that happens, in the very far future, though, artificial intelligence is a fascinating and growing field that is creating more jobs than it is taking away.

Artificial intelligence is intellect demonstrated by machines. This is in contrast to the natural intelligence of humans. With artificial intelligence, a system has the ability to interpret external data and learn from that data. It carries out tasks and achieves specific goals through flexible adaptation based on its learning. This is made possible using reasoning, probabilistic methods, statistical methods, artificial neural networks, and other approaches—but a physician doesn't necessarily need to be proficient in all of them to have a career in the field.

Machine learning is an application of artificial intelligence based on the idea that machines with access to the right data can use statistical models and algorithms to progressively improve their performance on specific tasks.

Artificial intelligence and machine learning are being applied to the health care industry for numerous processes, such as assisting providers in making diagnoses and choosing treatments, selecting appropriate drug dosages, and even decision-making during surgical procedures. They allow for complex medical data to be analyzed by approximating human cognition.

Artificial intelligence currently is used in health care primarily within radiology, telehealth, and clinical decision support applications. Major players in the technology industry, such as IBM, Microsoft, Intel, and Google, are actively involved in the artificial intelligence space, and the field is buzzing with medical startup companies. Furthermore, the U.S. government has invested in health care initiatives that rely on artificial intelligence.[15,16]

THE ROLE OF NONCLINICAL PHYSICIANS

At this time, physicians are most widely utilized within the artificial intelligence field to assist in revolutionizing clinical decision-making. Clinical decision support tools encompass certain types of documentation templates, contextually relevant reference information, and computerized alerts; however, they are becoming increasingly complex through the use of artificial intelligence.

Physicians are needed to ensure that solutions utilizing artificial intelligence and machine learning lead to appropriate medical care provision.

A physician's experience and expertise can ensure that medication management, treatment selection, medical data analysis, digital consultations, and health monitoring are carried out in ways that are safe and evidence-based. Any algorithms and underlying methodologies must be clinically accurate for the solution to be effective. Physicians can provide input up front, test for accuracy on the back end, and guide revisions and improvements.

Physicians are also in a prime position to identify new ways in which artificial intelligence can improve the medical field and patient care.

Employers
- Academic institution or university
- Clinical decision support solution provider
- Government agency
- Health tech startup
- Medical imaging analytics company
- Telehealth company

JOB SUMMARY—DIRECTOR OF CLINICAL DECISION SUPPORT

Similar Job Titles

- Clinical Strategist
- Director of Clinical Strategy
- Director of Medical Management
- Physician Clinical Support Analyst
- Physician Informaticist

A clinical decision support or clinical strategy director uses knowledge of medicine, epidemiology, clinical informatics, and health care delivery science to provide subject matter expertise in system design. Ultimately, the director provides medical perspective to assist the company in developing a product that a health care organization can use to balance quality and cost.

This role is likely to have involvement in the full product life cycle, including initial development, upgrades, implementation, training, and support activities. Physicians in this type of position are heavily involved in clinically validating that an algorithm or platform is functioning as intended and is clinically sound.

Depending on the organization, the director's work may be focused on a specific patient type, disease, or therapeutic area. Responsibilities may concentrate on underlying algorithms or on the tools that use those algorithms, either generally or in a specific care setting, such as telemedicine.

Example Responsibilities

- Provide clinical expertise to advance the practicality and effectiveness of the company's tools
- Develop manuscripts and presentations based on relevant research and data
- Offer improvements to a tool based on medical evidence and standards
- Form external partnerships to support product development and market uptake
- Collaborate with quality management teams to ensure product quality and safety

- Engage with customers to efficiently implement solutions and identify areas of need
- Train health care providers on product use
- Present initiatives to health care, governmental, or academic stakeholders

QUALIFICATIONS

Qualifications for physician positions depend on organization and product type as well as the position's responsibilities. A medical degree is required for some jobs, whereas a range of backgrounds can be suitable for others jobs that appeal to physicians due to the opportunity to use their knowledge in a unique way.

An interest in technologies and innovation in health care is a must. Research experience using complex health care data is beneficial. Coding language knowledge can be favorable, but is not routinely required.

COMPENSATION

Because artificial intelligence is a relatively new career area for physicians, it's difficult to provide any blanket statements about compensation. Nonetheless, it is fairly safe to say that companies who place value on a physician's skill sets will compensate well.

Director of Clinical Decision Support

19. Digital Health

Digital health encompasses any technologies and services that allow patients to improve their health without an in-person encounter or a trip to a clinic or hospital. This includes telehealth, mobile health (often referred to as mHealth), and wearable devices. Growth in this field has been swift, especially compared to that of traditional health care delivery.

Telehealth doesn't always involve the conventional format of a clinician on one video monitor and a patient on the other. It can be any service related to a person's health that is provided using an assistive technology. In addition to video conferencing, it encompasses sensors, remote monitoring, and other technologies.

At this time, mobile health is largely centered around smartphones. Simple mobile applications concentrate on personalized nutrition, sleep hygiene, mental wellness, and functional health and fitness. Complex mobile health solutions play into telehealth by providing a health care service remotely.

Wearable technology often is incorporated into health care by collecting human data and then analyzing and drawing conclusions based on that data. It has been described as "a check engine light for your body."[17] Although a wearable device's purpose can be as benign as estimating calories burned or tracking heart rate, the significance of these technologies should not be understated.

Many digital health companies are, at their core, focused on patient empowerment and self-management. They aim to make health convenient and accessible through mobile devices or the Internet. Through these services, patients learn disease triggers, lifestyle and behavioral management, and preventive measures.

As the range of digital health solutions broadens and their use becomes widespread, there is an increasing focus on efficiency, meeting patient preferences, and less expensive equipment. Digital health, along with the growth of "big data" at both personal and population levels, has the potential to effectively preserve health and manage disease.

THE ROLE OF NONCLINICAL PHYSICIANS

Digital health can make small-scale improvements in individuals' health and disease control, but has the capacity to lead to large-scale evolution in health care delivery and population health. Clearly, trained medical professionals have something to offer here. Digital health solutions are accompanied by nuances and challenges that establish a need for physician involvement in research and development, marketing, and business operations.

Physicians ensure that the functionality of digital health products aligns with the latest scientific evidence and standards of care in various health care delivery settings. They are heavily involved in clinical and observational studies to assess the need for digital health services and evaluate effects on health outcomes.

Many medical devices have the ability to communicate with or connect to digital health systems. This convergence of devices with consumer technologies raises questions about the type and extent of regulation that is needed to maintain patient safety. Although the precise role for regulatory bodies is not yet defined, the FDA has taken interest in digital health oversight. Physician involvement in this field helps to mold regulation and policies that will improve health and health care provision.

Employers
- Academic institution
- Medical device company
- Mobile app company
- Telehealth company

JOB SUMMARY—DIRECTOR OF CLINICAL DEVELOPMENT

Similar Job Titles
- Chief Health Officer
- Director of Clinical Science
- Medical Director

A director of clinical development takes on a broad function in carrying out clinically and medically related aspects of a digital health company's strategy. This individual may set high-level priorities to assist the business in realizing its vision.

Clinical development directors are tasked with ensuring that evidence-based decisions are made in planning, programming, and adhering to quality standards. They represent the business externally and advocate for digital health at the regional, national, or even international level.

Collaborations between academic institutions and digital health companies are common, and directors in this type of role are often responsible for identifying synergies between organizations and fostering these relationships.

For a fully developed product, responsibilities are similar to those assumed by physicians working in medical affairs for other types of medical product companies.

Example Responsibilities
- Provide advice and guidance as part of the research and development process
- Facilitate opportunities for collaborations within and outside of the industry
- Engage with stakeholders and potential clients to advocate the use of digital health solutions
- Communicate clinician and patient needs to operations, research and development, and other teams
- Review and provide insight for publications related to research or marketing
- Support compliance with relevant accrediting and regulating bodies

QUALIFICATIONS

As with many physician positions in technology-related fields, company needs vary considerably. Roles focused on research and development place high value on research experience, analytical proficiency, and health IT and informatics knowledge. Established companies or those focusing on later product lifestyle stages are more likely to seek out physicians with business acumen and an interest in representing the company externally.

COMPENSATION

Compensation depends on factors such as experience level and scope of job responsibilities. In this growing field, physicians have transferability and the potential for salary increases as they gain experience.

Director of Clinical Development

20. Business Development, Sales, and Marketing

Business development is the process of creating value for an organization through its relationships, partnerships, markets, and customers. It combines strategic analysis, sales, and marketing. The value created can be related to profitability, brand, or the company's product.

The scope of work of a business development team varies based on the type and stage of the company. In large, established companies, business development teams may be focused on building strategic relationships with other companies to identify areas to expand or build new products. At startup companies, business development involves identifying market opportunities, driving growth, and even managing intellectual properties.

Business development is combined with sales and marketing divisions in many organizations. In others, these areas are distinct, but work closely with one another to support common goals.

Depending on the organization, sales and marketing efforts can be directed toward other businesses, individual consumers, or the government.

Both sales and marketing can be outsourced. Marketing firms work with companies to build their brands. They strategize and manage key messaging, advertising campaigns, online presence, public relations, and various forms of media. Some firms specialize in a sector, such as health care or pharmaceuticals.

THE ROLE OF NONCLINICAL PHYSICIANS

Business development, sales, and marketing are important parts of a business in any industry. For physicians, though, the opportunity is naturally greatest in the health care industry.

Positions in this field have not traditionally been held by physicians; however, this is changing. As health care products and services become more complex and competition increases, the value of having a subject matter expert on the business development team increases as well. Innovative health care companies face the challenge of proving their product's value to physicians, health care executives, and decision-makers who are discerning, busy, and constrained by tight budgets.

Physician practices want to increase their revenue, cut their costs, enhance their images, and improve patient outcomes. Competition and governmental and payer requirements make it difficult to run a sustainable practice. Physicians who can navigate these challenges are an asset.

Not only is work in business development nonclinical, but it is yet another step removed from clinical decision-making compared with many popular nonclinical careers. Some physicians will find this field to be a happy medium between conventional medicine and leaving health care–related work entirely.

Employers
- Biotech company
- Health care company
- Health tech startup
- Marketing firm or agency

JOB SUMMARY—DIRECTOR OF BUSINESS DEVELOPMENT

Similar Job Titles
- Business Development Specialist
- Vice President of Business Development

A director of business development identifies opportunities for growth, improvement, and new markets and customers. The director meets frequently with the senior management team to review strategy and product pipeline updates.

Much of the job centers around external relationships, through finding prospective new clients, building relationships, and securing new contracts. Depending on the company, customers may be health systems, vendors, physicians, or patients.

Traveling throughout an assigned territory may be required to make personal contact with current and prospective client accounts, to promote products, and to ensure ongoing customer satisfaction. Customizing, reviewing, and discussing proposals with new clients also is a significant job component, often done in conjunction with the sales team.

Finally, business development directors review and update marketing materials, represent the company at exhibits and conferences, and keep internal teams informed of customer needs and trends.

Example Responsibilities

- Build relationships with health care leaders within a defined domain
- Identify potential new markets or segments
- Increase sales in existing markets by addressing customer needs and recognizing challenges
- Participate in meetings, presentations, and product demonstrations
- Offer credibility to physician and health care executive decision-makers
- Capture customer insights to support product improvements
- Coach and train sales staff on clinical information and data relating to the product
- Act as a thought leader in the community and industry

OTHER NONCLINICAL JOB OPTIONS

Business development positions explicitly requiring a medical degree may be titled Physician Executive, Physician Consultant, or Medical Director.

Sales jobs are fitting for some physicians who have a knack for selling. Marketing is a consideration for physicians with a mix of creative talent and analytical thinking.

QUALIFICATIONS

Although not common, jobs in business development and sales that require or prefer candidates with a medical background do exist. A company may require a medical degree when its success depends on forming relationships with physicians and turning them into customers, users, or proponents.

Many positions not requiring a medical degree are, nevertheless, great opportunities for physicians. The capacity to build strong relationships with fellow physicians and health care leaders, proficiency in keeping up with advances in medicine, knowledge of the health care regulatory and financing landscapes, and comfort in presenting scientific information are valuable.

COMPENSATION

On average, business development director salaries are lower than those of clinical physicians. In any role that brings a company new business, however, there is the potential for compensation that is tied to meeting objectives. Sales jobs, in particular, often are commission-based. This makes it possible for some physicians to earn a total income that rivals that of clinical work.

Salary often is commensurate with previous experience. Health care or clinical experience is likely to count toward this experience, provided it is relevant to the company's product.

Director of Business Development

PHYSICIAN PROFILE:

Adam Travis, MD

JOB TITLE: Vice President of Provider Solutions

EMPLOYER: Clarify Health Solutions

What does your organization do?

My company offers machine learning and artificial intelligence–enabled predictive analytics and precision care guidance software-as-a-service applications for health care organizations.

What is your role within the organization?

I oversee product management for our software solutions targeted to health systems and physician groups.

What are your responsibilities?

My responsibilities encompass product strategy, commercial materials development, sales support, customer implementation support, and technical development road mapping.

What does a typical day on the job look like?

My average day is a mix of three types of activities and interactions: internal product management; customer delivery support; and business development support.

For product management, I work closely with our technical leadership to discuss proposed development roadmaps and assess feasibility of proposed enhancements to our offerings.

For customer delivery, I interface heavily with teams that implement our software and train customers on using our solution to ensure that they understand its full capabilities and ensure customer feedback is taken into account in guiding our ongoing development.

For business development, I support our sales team by providing technical expertise and input on pitch presentations and on proposals.

How does your medical background and experience contribute to your work?

Overall, my background is essential to both informing product strategy and understanding the "art of possible" with health data and where data limitations affect our ability to build new applications.

With regard to informing product strategy, my medical background allows me to understand, in a very nuanced way, our end customers and what problems they're really trying to solve in day-to-day care and clinical operations management that can be addressed with our offerings. In that sense, my medical background is a constant touch-stone for me in setting product strategy.

Understanding the full life cycle of health data allows me to effectively guide the development of new applications using our accumulated data. My medical background allows me to recognize the true meaning and significance of health data, because I have firsthand experience with the elements that should carry significance to whatever question we're trying to answer and the potential limitations and "red herrings" that can reside in health data.

What are the best parts of your job?

Medical practice was never a fit for me, because I was always far more intrigued with solving the broader system problems inherent in U.S. health care than I was with solving the problems of an individual patient. By working to bring state-of-the-art advanced analytics approaches into health care, I am, in effect, working to broadly improve the quality and efficiency of health care. This is a driving source of motivation for me.

What are the main challenges you face?

In many cases, we are building applications that many of our health system customers are not yet properly organized to use effectively, which means they often struggle with understanding or achieving the promised value from our solutions. Thus, perhaps the greatest challenge is finding partners that are willing to consider how to modify their current practices and roles to best use our solutions.

Where might your career go from here?

I am passionate about building analytics and artificial intelligence tools for use in health care, and so I hope to stay in a product management role in this field for the foreseeable future.

What are some considerations for physicians interested in a career in health technologies?

A deep understanding of end customer use is critical. Most physicians have this due to their medical training.

Experience in complex project management gained through administrative leadership positions or other "business" roles also is critical. This experience can be gained in multiple ways. I worked in health care management consulting after completing residency, which allowed me to build strong project management and team management skills. These have been valuable in my current role.

Some familiarity with data analysis and basic computer programming is helpful, whether acquired through research roles, prior education, or business experience. My undergraduate background in engineering, research projects throughout my education, and four years in consulting sharpened my analytical skills and fluency with data and statistics.

I would advise anyone considering a transition to ask themselves what really motivates them. If solving ambiguous problems without any "textbook" answers, spending time managing teams rather than individually executing work, and building tools or products that less directly (but much more broadly) benefit health care is more appealing than individual clinical practice, many jobs in health technology may be a good fit.

Professional and Financial Services

The service sector (also known as the tertiary sector) of the economy involves the provision of intangible activities or benefits to the customer. Professional services are provided by specially trained individuals and often require a license. Conventional medical practice is, of course, a professional service; however, there is a need for medical expertise in other service fields.

Any service businesses with health care companies as clients or whose activities tangentially involve patients, health organizations, biomedical companies, or health care workers can benefit from physician involvement. These include financial, legal, insurance, and consulting services.

Professional services industries have been affected by technology developments. In some cases, these developments have substantially changed the way that services are offered and have altered client expectations. Service businesses touching the health care industry rely on professionals' understanding of patient care processes, health care delivery and payment models, and emerging medical science.

21. Management Consulting

Management consulting is the process of creating value for organizations through advisory and implementation services. This may sound vague. Indeed, the field is broad. It is dominated by the multibillion dollar firms McKinsey, Boston Consulting Group, and Bain & Company, which together are colloquially referred to as the "Big Three" of management consulting. There are many other important players in the industry, as well.

Client organizations hire management consulting firms to improve strategy development, organization performance, or operational processes. Client engagements are focused on a specific question, problem, or goal that the company has. For example, a business may seek direction on its functional strategy or assistance in determining whether a merger or acquisition would be favorable to them.

From an operational standpoint, a consulting firm might assist a client with outsourcing strategy, approach to marketing, or supply chain schema. Consulting firms also work with clients on compensation models and organizational-level changes aimed at improving overall performance.

Some firms—especially the large ones—offer extensive services across a wide range of industries. Others focus on particular industries, such as retail, electronics, medical products, or the social sector. Clients may be for-profit, not-for-profit, or government entities.

Some management consulting companies offer technology solutions, enterprise systems, and other services that are packaged with their consulting services.

The term *business consulting* often is used interchangeably with *management consulting,* although it tends to focus more on the operational and production levels within a small or startup business.

THE ROLE OF NONCLINICAL PHYSICIANS

The role of most physicians in management consulting is similar to that of non-MD management consultants. Client engagements are completed by small teams made up of consultants with a variety of backgrounds and degrees. The team members' consulting experience may be the only thing they have in common. Therefore, a medical degree is advantageous in an indirect way.

Like medicine, consulting is part art and part science. This is one reason it tends to appeal to doctors. Medical knowledge and experience in a health care setting can influence the way client problems are approached, how issues are considered, and what solutions are implemented.

Due to their backgrounds, physicians commonly work on projects in the health care, biotech, pharmaceutical, and medical product industries. Those new to consulting, though, may be assigned to engagements that are unrelated to health care.

Consulting requires listening, investigating, recommending, collaborating, and implementing. The physician's scientific knowledge, patient care experience, and health care delivery system understanding impart a unique perspective for each aspect of consulting work.

Employers
- Full-service management consulting firm
- Strategy consulting firm

JOB SUMMARY—ASSOCIATE CONSULTANT

Similar Job Titles
- Associate
- Business Analyst
- Business Consultant

Physicians entering the consulting field often enter as an associate in the firm. They are dedicated to a single client engagement at any one time. Team structure can vary, but a typical team includes an engagement manager, two or three associates, and a business analyst.

Over the course of the engagement, associate consultants spend much of their time at the client site. A standard day varies based on the project, but might include interviewing client leadership, analyzing data, performing research, updating team members on progress, and developing deliverables.

Between client engagements, associate consultants can be involved in internal projects, recruiting efforts, and providing subject matter expertise to ongoing engagements.

Example Responsibilities
- Perform analyses to solve complex business problems
- Summarize large quantities of information and identify trends and key findings
- Provide an outside perspective on major business decisions for clients
- Glean information from company data and staff interviews
- Travel to company sites to work on engagements
- Keep up with industry trends relating to ongoing engagements
- Develop executive-level reports and oral presentations for clients

OTHER NONCLINICAL JOB OPTIONS

Physicians who want to stay in the management consulting field after working for a couple of years as an associate can be promoted to Engagement Manager or Project Leader. Positions surpassing that level include firm partner and principal.

QUALIFICATIONS

For some firms, simply having a medical degree carries weight. It demonstrates intelligence, broad science knowledge, learning ability, and—for better or worse—the willingness to work long, arduous hours.

Strong analytical ability is a must. It is common for firms to require candidates to complete a written test and case-based interviews to demonstrate this skill.

Extensive business knowledge is not required. Firms are willing to train otherwise solid candidates on the business skills needed to succeed. This training may be informal or may be part of an official program or new hire training.

COMPENSATION

In most cases, salary starts out lower than what physicians can make in clinical practice; the difference fades, however, for those who excel at consulting and stick with it.

Many management consulting firms have standard pay structures with little room for negotiation. But generous bonuses and hefty increases accompany promotion. Promotions can be offered quickly for high performers.

The travel burden of consulting is not for everyone. Those who enjoy it, however, will appreciate the chance to see new places and rack up airline miles and hotel status.

The nonmonetary value of working as a consultant is considerable. Physicians employed by well-regarded consulting firms are rewarded with large professional networks and great career opportunities.

Associate Consultant

Engagement Manager

22. Health Care Consulting

Health care organizations turn to external resources for more than operational needs. They do so to support vision, control costs, or find innovative solutions to challenges or questions they face. Demand for health care consulting has been rising due to an increasingly complex health system and the need for changes in the way care is delivered in order for health care organizations to maintain profitability or remain competitive.

Health care consulting firm clients cover the breadth of the health care industry. Hospitals hire health care consultants to adjust to changing regulations, adopt technologies, and make strategic decisions in response to economic and industry trends. Physician practices and outpatient centers use health care consulting services for financial management and to improve efficiency of services provided.

Health care consultants are being called on by government clients to address increasing expenditures as they relate to factors such as the aging population. For example, health insurance companies rely on consultants to identify ways to implement care management tools and effectively utilize health care analytics. Nonprofits, medical laboratories, and other health-related organizations make up a portion of health care consulting firm clients, as well.

In contrast to the large, well-known management consulting players, health care consulting companies are specialist or "boutique" firms that concentrate on distinct areas or types of organizations. Some focus on one of the industry sectors described earlier, offering a breadth of services. Others have clients across the health care industry, but specialize in a niches, such as financial management or IT strategy.

Another distinguishing feature of health care consulting companies is that they are more likely than management consulting firms to play a role in implementing the recommendations they make. Implementation may come in the form of a process change, new technology, provider training, or other solution.

THE ROLE OF NONCLINICAL PHYSICIANS

Health care consulting hits closer to home for many physicians than generalist management consulting. Client sites are familiar settings. Engagements are related to topics that many physicians have directly or tangentially been involved with, through their own practices, hospital leadership positions, or serving on committees and task forces.

Engagements focusing on both discrete operational issues and big-picture strategic challenges require medical knowledge and experience, to varying degrees.

Health care consultants must interact with administrative and medical leadership within client organizations. This can be easier for physicians than for consultants of other backgrounds. Physicians have the advantage of firsthand experience in working through the challenges faced by a health care company. They can often build relationships faster and more easily garner respect from staff of client companies.

Physicians can use their medical expertise to ensure that patients' best interest is kept in mind through all recommendations and decisions made by the consulting team.

Employers
- Health care boutique consulting firm
- Management consulting firm

JOB SUMMARY—HEALTH CARE CONSULTANT

Similar Job Titles
- Associate
- Physician Consultant
- Subject Expert

Health care consultants conduct formal engagements for client organizations. They create strategies and recommendations for the client, sometimes taking steps to implement them. Most days are spent at client sites.

Consultants spend much of their time on strategic management, in which they advise the organization on overall direction. To do so, they analyze data, define and measure problems, interview stakeholders, act as medical and clinical subject matter experts, and deliver presentations. They also write proposals and produce status updates.

Consultants work as external change agents, figuring out how health care organizations can adopt and adapt to remain afloat in the health care industry. Tasks may incorporate aspects of process improvement, such as Six Sigma, root cause analysis, and quality management.

For health IT projects, consultants provide support related to IT product selection and implementation, product and device interfaces, and software use for analytics purposes.

Financial management is another significant part of the job for many health care consultants. Financial engagements may focus on negotiating vendor contracts, improving claims processes, or identifying new cost-effective patient services.

Example Responsibilities

- Identify, research, and analyze performance indicators and metrics
- Leverage operational and financial data to improve client organization performance
- Ensure that client deliverables are of high quality and accuracy
- Lead meetings and presentations for senior client leadership
- Oversee the design and implementation of recommended solutions
- Work with client leadership to take action on recommendations
- Develop reports on project methodologies, findings, and recommendations

OTHER NONCLINICAL JOB OPTIONS

Physicians who work their way up within a health care consulting firm take on the titles of Manager or Principal, which are accompanied by both increasing compensation and increasing responsibility.

QUALIFICATIONS

Consulting firms appreciate physician consultants who have a combination of health care experience and business acumen. Depending on the consulting firm's focus area, experience in other areas may be needed, such as health care revenue cycle management or managed care products.

Most health care consultants are not physicians. Board certification and a medical license are not needed.

COMPENSATION

Compensation for consultants at niche health care consulting firms may be somewhat lower than that of top-tier generalist management consulting companies. Nonetheless, smaller companies are more likely to have flexibility in the salaries they offer, based on the skills and experience that physician consultants bring to the table.

Generous bonus structures are common, and can be based on both individual performance and company sales.

Frequent travel, which is commonplace in health care consulting, is a benefit for some but a drawback for others. Some firms, though, focus their efforts within a limited geographic area.

Health Care Consultant

23. Investment Banking, Private Equity, and Venture Capital

Investment banks trade stocks and other securities, research and offer outlooks on financial markets, and provide advice to client corporations. They often are referred to as the "sell side" of the investment banking industry. Investment banking is not truly banking or investment; rather, it is the business of raising capital for companies and advising them from a financial perspective. They generate revenue through fees and commissions. Whereas large investment banks offer a full range of services, many boutique organizations focus on advisory roles.

Alternatively, the "buy side" of the industry refers to institutional investors or asset managers who buy the securities recommended by the sell side. These companies can be private equity firms, hedge funds, mutual funds, or other fund types. The buy side aims to make money through growth in the value of its investments.

A private equity firm is an investment company that provides capital in exchange for ownership stake in a private company. The firm manages the investing activities associated with their private equity fund in exchange for a management fee and percentage of profits generated. Many investments are made in the early stages of a company, though funds sometimes invest in established companies in what is known as a leveraged buyout.

Venture capital is a type of private equity typically provided to early-stage companies with a high potential for growth. Because investing in these companies may be seen as too risky for standard capital markets or bank loans, the fund is a pooled investment from third-party investors. The funds profit when the funded company is sold or made public through an initial public offering (IPO). Some venture capital funds target specific technologies or sectors.

THE ROLE OF NONCLINICAL PHYSICIANS

Both sides of the investment industry must make careful, informed decisions about investing activities to keep afloat. As a result, the professionals involved in making these decisions are key. Professionals with a specialized body of knowledge are needed to predict stock moves and company outlooks as accurately as possible. Not many professions scream "specialized body of knowledge" quite like medicine.

Much of the legwork completed before an investment decision or recommendation is made involves researching the relevant industry, field, company, and competitors. Investment banks typically are organized by industry, so physicians tend to be hired by firms that focus on or have divisions dedicated to biotechnology or health care.

Given the complexities of the drug and biotechnology development processes, physicians are well-positioned to interpret clinical data and make predictions about a company's market position or future clinical success.

In clinical work, reading about current therapeutic landscapes and advances in medicine is necessary in order to maintain an evidence-based practice. In the financial industry, this ever-changing knowledge is used to convince others to buy or sell securities. Physicians have the ability to stay updated on relevant news from scientific, regulatory, clinical, and commercial outlets.

Employers
- Investment bank
- Investment research firm
- Private equity firm

JOB SUMMARY—BIOTECHNOLOGY EQUITY RESEARCH ASSOCIATE

Similar Job Titles
- Investment Analyst
- Stock Research Associate
- Venture Capital Associate

Equity researchers review companies and write prospective reports. This information is used to assist traders, investment bankers, and fund managers in their decisions, thereby generating revenue for them.

An associate starts the day by getting up to speed on news and press releases within the industry segment of interest. This involves digesting a large volume of information and determining how it may affect the organization's covered stocks or investment decisions. To illustrate, a press release highlighting the completion of an investigational drug's phase 3 clinical trial may increase the probability of success that is used in calculating financial estimates for the drug company.

The remainder of the (usually quite long) day involves meetings to discuss findings and investments, preparing presentations, pitching ideas to clients, and performing financial modeling and valuation work.

Example Responsibilities
- Analyze and prepare financial statements
- Develop models to project a company's future financial performance
- Conduct industry and company research
- Keep informed of industry and market developments
- Attend medical and scientific conferences to keep abreast of research directions
- Meet with clients and industry professionals
- Identify and contact potential buyers and investors

OTHER NONCLINICAL JOB OPTIONS

There is a hierarchy in equity research. Analysts do the equivalent of "scut work" in the finance world by performing research, modeling, and summarizing findings in reports. Many physicians entering the field do so as associates, a position that includes similar work to that of analysts but with more responsibility, such as a focus on strategy and client-facing time. From there, standard promotions are to senior associate, followed by vice president, then partner or managing director.

Professionals in the finance industry can shift their careers between the buy side and the sell side and between company types. A physician with experience in venture capital, for example, is well positioned to work for a hedge fund or perform equity research.

Physicians with an interest in finance also may find fulfillment in corporate finance. The scope of work for a chief financial officer, vice president of finance, or other corporate finance position varies greatly, depending on company size and type. At a health technology startup, a corporate finance role may involve finding and securing funding sources, budget planning, forming financial projections, and developing overall financial strategy.

QUALIFICATIONS

A medical degree is not required to work in investment banking or private equity. Analysts often are hired directly out of undergrad, and many associates have MBAs or PhDs. Depending on the firm's needs, an MD behind your name may or may not carry weight. More substantial are analytical ability and an understanding of finance.

The Financial Industry Regulatory Authority (FINRA) oversees licensing and exams related to securities activities. One or more licenses may be required for positions in this field.

A research background—especially in translational research—can be helpful.

A willingness to work long hours is a must. Work weeks of 80 to 100 hours are commonplace for analysts and associates.

COMPENSATION

Similar to management consulting, promotions up a standard organizational hierarchy are accompanied by increasing responsibility and income. Base salaries for analysts and associates may not be negotiable. Bonuses make up a hefty percentage of overall compensation. Bonus structure can be complex, depending on performance of stocks under coverage, trading activity, business revenues, performance evaluations, and institutional investor rankings.

Associate positions can require substantial travel to meet with clients.

For those who learn quickly, put in the effort, and establish themselves as a dedicated group member within the firm, the financial reward can be huge.

Biotechnology Equity Research Associate

24. Wealth Management and Private Banking

Wealth management combines financial planning, investment management, and other financial services. It is meant to address essentially all aspects of a client's finances in a comprehensive, packaged service. When the client is a high-net-worth individual, this is known as *private wealth management*. Consumers of this service can also be organizations, such as small businesses, foundations, and endowments.

Private banking provides a similar array of offerings, although it typically is offered by a commercial bank, in addition to traditional banking services, to customers who meet a minimum threshold of assets under management.

Although the basic principles of wealth management stand the test of time, the industry is evolving. Client preferences and expectations are being shaped by new technologies, economic crises, and other circumstances. New business models for wealth management companies have emerged to help them remain competitive in the information age. Moreover, as with the health care industry, increasing regulatory burdens demand that organizations adapt to stay afloat.

Use of analytics and algorithms is on the rise in this field, resulting in tools such as "robo advisors." These are felt by some to be market disrupters, but often work synergistically with traditional wealth management services.

THE ROLE OF NONCLINICAL PHYSICIANS

This is a field in which a physician's knowledge of biology and medicine is unlikely to be exceptionally useful. However, use of other elements of their experience and skills make this a desirable nonclinical career for some physicians.

Medical school graduates emerge with a boatload of debt, but quickly become high-income earners upon completing residency. Physicians who have been proactive about optimizing their financial situations have firsthand experience in how to invest and manage wealth.

Although physicians sometimes are targeted by wealth managers due to a perception that they are financially unsavvy, most excel at hard skills, such as math and science, and have the capacity to become proficient in financial concepts.

Wealth management is far from just hard skills, though. We all recognize how a good bedside manner, ability to empathize, and a knack for delivering bad news can contribute to developing a good relationship with patients. Similarly, a financial advisor's success is highly dependent on a strong relationship with clients. Trust, dependability, and solid communication are key.

Another parallel to clinical practice is the need to balance risk versus expected benefit. All financial investments carry risk. Successful wealth management requires an understanding of the fundamental drivers of investments. Professionals in this field must pay attention to and question the context and repercussions of current events, new technologies, and cultural and social trends.

Firms with a physician in the role of wealth manager or financial advisor may appeal to prospective clients who are doctors because they trust another physician to fully understand their financial situation.

Employers
- Financial services company
- Investment or commercial bank
- Wealth management firm

JOB SUMMARY—WEALTH MANAGEMENT ADVISOR

Similar Job Titles
- Client Strategist
- Financial Advisor
- Private Wealth Management Associate

- Wealth Manager

A wealth management advisor creates wealth management plans that are designed to address individualized goals for the client. To varying degrees, advisors also carry out the plan—for example, by buying or selling stocks.

Advisors must determine the best asset allocation for a client, with asset classes including fixed income, stocks, and equities. Many high-net-worth individuals desire assistance with selecting and executing alternative investments, such as real assets, direct investments with startups and private companies, or hedge funds. This is accomplished using projections that rely on the client's financial goals.

A wealth advisor's services often exceed conventional investment advice. They may include developing overarching life goals and aspects of long-term planning that may influence financial decisions.

Some tasks are similar to those of an associate in private equity or investment banking, because many clients have the means to invest large amounts across several asset classes. Private wealth management advisors working for commercial banks can leverage the organization's resources to increase the value they offer to clients.

Example Responsibilities
- Strategize to help clients achieve their financial goals
- Analyze financial information
- Stay updated on changes to client needs and goals
- Develop strong relationships with clients
- Conduct client portfolio review meetings
- Manage client assets to help achieve financial goals
- Identify opportunities with new and existing clients to increase market presence and client base
- Work with colleagues to enhance and elevate the firm's efficiency and profitability

QUALIFICATIONS

In terms of formal education, most wealth management advisor positions require only a bachelor's degree.

An advanced understanding of investments and the skill to communicate them to clients is needed. Because advisors often are expected to bring in new clients to the firm, business development and marketing skills are important.

Numerous certifications are relevant to wealth managers, one or more of which may be required or preferred for certain roles. Common certifications include Certified Financial Planner (CFP), Certified Private Wealth Advisor (CPWA), and Chartered Financial Analyst (CFA).

One or more FINRA licenses also may be required.

COMPENSATION

Salary is only one component of compensation for wealth advisors. Bonuses and commissions are common, and can exceed base pay for many positions—especially those with seniority. As a result, the range for total compensation is large.

Wealth Management Advisor

25. Medical Law

Physicians are acutely aware of the importance of law in medicine. Many, however, prefer to keep their distance from the subject of law, associating it with malpractice lawsuits and regulations that interfere with the ability to focus on patients.

Law is more than these unwanted effects on clinical practice, however. It is intertwined with every aspect of medicine and health care. Medical law concerns the rights and responsibilities of medical professionals and their patients. Health law further incorporates law as it relates to health insurance companies, pharmaceuticals and medical products, clinical research, and other disciplines that ultimately impact patients' lives.

A career integrating medicine with law can incorporate medical malpractice, corporate transactions and financing, regulation, privacy and consent, and medical ethics. The complexities of health care delivery and payment have led to increasing demand for legal experts.

THE ROLE OF NONCLINICAL PHYSICIANS

Professionals in medical law are advisors and advocates of their clients. As advisors, they assist individual or organizational clients in understanding their obligations, legal rights, and appropriate courses of action. As advocates, they represent, review, and present evidence in support of clients. Physicians are in a unique position to take on these roles, having firsthand experience in health care settings and a solid knowledge of medicine.

Physicians can skillfully review medical documentation, interpret medical test results, and understand clinical situations in the context of scientific evidence. When combined with an understanding of relevant law and regulation, this is a considerable asset to a company or individual facing legal challenges.

Employers
- Corporation in a health-related field

- Hospital or health care system
- Law firm

JOB SUMMARY—DIRECTOR OF RISK MANAGEMENT AND COMPLIANCE

Similar Job Titles

- Chief Risk and Compliance Officer
- Corporate Compliance Director
- Director of Ethics, Privacy, and Compliance
- Risk Management Expert
- Risk Manager

Physicians in risk management positions advise organizations on how to minimize or eliminate risk. Those in compliance positions work to ensure that the organization and its personnel are complying with all applicable laws and regulations, as well as with internal policies and procedures. Given the overlap of these functions, they're often combined into a single leadership position.

A director of risk management and compliance stays informed about various laws, regulations, rules, and codes that are applicable to the company's product or service. For a hospital system, these may be related to incident reporting, patient care and safety, and medical claims and billing. A similar role at a pharmaceutical company may focus on matters related to safety reporting, post-marketing commitments to the FDA, facility inspections, and standard operating procedures.

Example Responsibilities

- Develop and implement company policies and procedures that affect liability exposures
- Conduct systems analysis to identify patterns that could result in compensable events
- Design risk mitigation strategies and activities
- Respond to deficiencies identified by regulatory bodies or insurance companies
- Advise clinicians regarding disclosure conversations and their documentation
- Plan and coordinate risk financing and insurance programs

- Make recommendations to general counsel relating to claim activities
- Provide education to company staff and promote a culture of compliance
- Maintain up-to-date knowledge of industry organizations and regulatory bodies

JOB SUMMARY—LAW FIRM ASSOCIATE

Similar Job Titles

- Lawyer
- Attorney

In response to the changes and complexities of the health care delivery landscape, it has become common for attorneys specializing in medical law to subspecialize within their practices. Physician attorneys may find a niche in a law firm specializing in health care law or a large, multispecialty firm with a medical division. A firm's scope of practice can be broad, covering medical malpractice, corporate transactions, health technologies, administrative law, health care reimbursement matters, and other aspects of health law.

Law firm associates often have the opportunity to work with clients in a range of industry sectors, such as medical groups, hospitals, health care payers, and biopharmaceutical companies.

Law firm attorneys focusing on medical malpractice are primarily responsible for representing hospitals, health care professionals, or patients in medical liability actions.

Example Responsibilities

- Perform medical and legal research
- Draft and respond to discovery motions
- Take and defend depositions
- Appear in court
- Review and analyze documentation and evidence for legal proceedings
- Provide status reports to clients

OTHER NONCLINICAL JOB OPTIONS

In addition to law firms, the combination of an MD and JD is fitting for employment with health care organizations in the position of general counsel, corporate counsel, or chief legal officer. Companies requiring an in-house counsel span all sectors of the health care industry and also include government agencies and academic institutions.

CONSULTING OPPORTUNITIES IN MEDICAL LAW

The majority of physicians professionally involved in medical law do so as independent contractors rather than full-time employees. Expert witness work involves reviewing medical records and other information related to legal matters and developing a medical opinion regarding care that a patient received or management that a clinician provided. It can involve giving depositions and appearing in trial.

Expert witnesses are consultants to law firms, and lawyers are heavily involved in the cases. Consequently, the physician expert is not usually required to have a thorough knowledge of the law. Although expert witnesses are not full-time employees, physicians with ample clinical experience and distinct areas of medical expertise may be able to find enough consulting opportunities to replace their salaries through expert witness work.

QUALIFICATIONS

Many leadership positions in risk management and compliance in health-related sectors are open to individuals with a variety of credentials. Medical professionals with an interest in and knowledge of relevant law can be candidates, even without formal law training.

Some employers may place value on certification by one of several risk management certification bodies. A knowledge of legal requirements and regulatory codes as they relate to the company's line of work is required. Experience in process improvement and strategic planning and implementation is a plus.

Physicians who obtain a JD degree have the most options within medical law. Law school is a three-year program, and graduates must pass a bar examination in order to practice law. This is a big commitment. After completing medical school and residency and taking the USMLE and board exams, however, it may not seem like such a massive undertaking to physicians looking for a career change or who miss being actively engaged in learning.

The necessary experience for a law firm attorney position can be gained during internships and other practical experiences during law school.

Experience working in health care is a plus for attorneys vying for health and medical sector general counsel positions. Other required experience and expertise depends on company type and stage, as well as where their legal needs lie.

COMPENSATION

Salaries in risk management and compliance vary based on multiple factors, such as organization size and position scope.

Although average salaries are somewhat lower for lawyers than physicians, lawyers are compensated well. Law firm pay structures often incentivize upward movement within the firm, with considerable increases accompanying promotions. A law firm associate normally doesn't hold ownership interest in the firm, whereas partners earn a portion of profits and have voting rights.

Director of Risk Management and Compliance

Law Firm Associate

26. Life Insurance Industry

Life insurance companies are in the market of providing financial remuneration to beneficiaries when the policyholder dies. Although the top dozen companies account for close to half of the industry's assets, there are over 2000 life insurance companies in the United States.[18] Their revenue is generated from both member premiums and asset investment. Many also offer an array of other financial services.

Life insurance products include term life, whole life, and group life. These vary by the coverage length, benefit type, and pricing structure. Customers are charged a monthly premium calculated using details such as their age and health status.

Upon receiving an application for life insurance from a prospective policyholder, an underwriting process is used to classify the applicant's risk. The applicant may be a group (such as an employer) or an individual. Insurers use a variety of processes and data in their underwriting decisions. Applicants are clustered into categories according to mortality risk. If it is determined that insurance can be issued, additional analysis determines the correct premium rate to apply to the policy.

Claims adjustment is the process of investigating the circumstances of policyholder death, determining eligibility under the terms of the contract, and actually paying the claim.

THE ROLE OF NONCLINICAL PHYSICIANS

On the surface, the need for physicians in this industry seems minor. The number of physicians is quite small compared to other types of professionals in the field, but medical professionals play an important role.

As opposed to conventional clinical medicine, in which physicians treat illness to improve outcomes and quality of life, physicians in the life insurance industry use medical data to evaluate mortality risk. A person applying for life insurance must disclose relevant medical history, which is best interpreted by a medical professional.

Prognosis is rarely obvious from a summarized medical history. Physicians must determine the implications of abnormal radiographic findings, electrocardiograms, pulmonary function tests, urinalyses, and other data. They assess the extent of the impact that smoking, cancer, or cardiac disease has on risk of death, in the context of an individual's demographics and medical history.

A life expectancy estimation—in part determined by a physician's review— allows the company to make a decision about the risk they're taking on.

Employer
- Life insurance company

JOB SUMMARY—LIFE INSURANCE MEDICAL DIRECTOR

Similar Job Title
- Vice President of Medical Management

Life insurance medical directors provide consultative medical services to the company's underwriting and claims divisions. The insurer takes on financial risk with each product issued, and relies on physicians to weigh decisions about risk versus benefit.

Medical directors are in a position of authority. Their work combines clinical knowledge, statistics, and data interpretation. They spend much of their time providing expert medical opinion based on medical data and record review. Their decisions during the underwriting process can affect the number of claims that the company receives in the future.

When a claim is made, the medical director opines on the cause of death and the presence of undisclosed medical conditions—factors that may affect whether a benefit is paid to the policyholder's beneficiary. This task can be complicated by incomplete medical reports and uninformative death certificates.

Medical directors are expected to be up to date in relevant medical science to reach sound determinations, as well as to strike a balance between being fair to the applicant or policyholder and making a strong financial decision for the company.

In addition to reviewing individual cases, medical directors are involved in wider company initiatives and strategizing. Companies considering a new product or line of business involve medical directors in the planning stages to develop risk rating systems, underwriting processes and workflows, and even marketing approaches. Medical directors may be involved in educating staff regarding medically-related topics.

Example Responsibilities
- Provide consultations and assessments to underwriters and claims analysts
- Interpret electrocardiograms and other diagnostic tests
- Review medical literature as it relates to changes in mortality
- Provide ongoing review and revision of underwriting processes and policies
- Maintain current knowledge of medical literature and guidelines
- Visit field offices to educate and train staff and consultants on medical aspects of underwriting
- Participate in committees and policy development

QUALIFICATIONS

Clinical experience is important for life insurance medical director positions. Physicians in this role must be comfortable reviewing and interpreting medical test results and clinical data. A medical degree and board certification typically are required, and an active medical license may be required in some cases.

COMPENSATION

Compensation can be comparable to that of clinical work, but with the added bonuses of regular hours during a standard work week and no on-call requirements. There is far less sense of urgency in the case of a death than is experienced in a patient care setting.

Life Insurance Medical Director

27. Disability Insurance Industry

Disability takes a toll in the United States. Over a quarter of adults in the United States have a disability.[19] The unemployment rate for the disabled population is more than twice that of Americans without a disability.[20] Securing short-term and long-term disability insurance is a priority for many workers when starting a job.

Compared with the health insurance marketplace, the disability insurance industry is operated by a relatively small number of organizations and has shown a trend toward consolidation. Like health insurance companies, disability insurance providers look for solutions to improve the services they offer to members while simultaneously controlling costs.

Disability insurance underwriting is the process used to evaluate an applicant and place that person into a broad category according to morbidity expectations. A number of factors weigh into this assessment, including demographics, occupation, and income level, although the most important is health. The assigned category determines whether a policy will be issued and the details of that policy.

An effective underwriting process is imperative, because disability claims can be a substantial expense for the company. Accurately evaluating claim risk up front can mitigate loss down the road.

Claims investigation begins with a claims specialist performing an initial review and verifying the individual's eligibility. It then aims to determine whether disability is present by reviewing the claimant's current loss and functional level. Anticipated disability duration and likelihood of returning to work are evaluated.

Underwriting and claims review for disability insurance is substantially different than that for life insurance. Disability insurance underwriting considers morbidity rather than mortality risk. Certain medical issues that affect decisions made by a life insurance provider may have little significance when it comes to disability insurance.

THE ROLE OF NONCLINICAL PHYSICIANS

Disability insurance companies need the infrastructure to address any application and claim situation. Medical professionals are a key part of this.

Physicians are able to identify conditions or impairments that should not be covered or have reduced coverage in future claims, as well as to accurately assess medical data as part of claim reviews.

Similar to case reviews for utilization management jobs, the physician's role in disability underwriting and claims investigations relies heavily on medical knowledge and the ability to interpret and apply scientific evidence.

Disability insurance companies are increasingly emphasizing member health and productive lifestyles—another area in which physician involvement is needed. Many companies offer support services to members in an effort to rehabilitate and enable them to return to work. This can include making referrals to clinical programs, providing mental health resources, and offering medical consultations to ensure that treatment plans are appropriate.

Employer
- Disability insurance company

JOB SUMMARY—DISABILITY INSURANCE MEDICAL DIRECTOR

Similar Job Titles
- Medical Review Officer
- Physician Consultant

Disability insurance medical directors are tasked with providing direction and medical expertise on both individual member cases and larger projects and company initiatives.

Responsibilities that are medically focused occur during the underwriting process, claim investigation, and other aspects of the disability insurance service lifecycle. Medical directors review and interpret member records, perform risk assessments, assist in projecting medical costs, and apply medical literature to cases.

Medical reviews involve basic clinical data, such as height and weight, medications, and medical history. Some medical conditions require that more detailed data be closely examined. These include musculoskeletal disorders, heart conditions, neurologic conditions, and conditions and complications related to pregnancy. Medical directors may need to consult with external physicians regarding the member's medical treatment.

From a strategy standpoint, medical directors may develop initiatives focused on functional restoration and return-to-work. They may apply analytical techniques to determine how underwriting processes can be improved.

Example Responsibilities

- Review applications, examinations, laboratory and test results, and medical records
- Provide medical analysis of claims files and underwriting applications
- Consult with and educate legal, underwriting, compliance, and product development staff on clinical topics
- Apply medical knowledge to determine functional capacity and impairment
- Apply federal and state regulations and company policies to medical assessments
- Assess the accuracy of diagnosis, treatment plans, and prognosis through medical record review
- Develop policies and processes to evaluate applications and claims from a medical standpoint
- Liaise with medical consultants and external physicians

OTHER NONCLINICAL JOB OPTIONS

Disability insurance sales is another career option. Doctors represent an entire market within the disability insurance industry, due to high income and the physical and mental ability needed to practice medicine.

Doctors also tend to think (or are told) that they have unique financial and insurance needs. Physicians can be quite successful selling disability insurance to peers due to being relatable and empathetic in the sales process.

CONSULTING OPPORTUNITIES IN THE DISABILITY INSURANCE INDUSTRY

Disability insurance companies often use independent medical exams (IMEs) to determine disability or functional level. Physicians performing IMEs typically are consultants who are compensated on a per-review basis. The work involves a clinical component, because in-person exams often are needed. Nonetheless, some physicians will find that the work is sufficiently removed from traditional clinical medicine. Others may choose to conduct IMEs to gain experience and strengthen candidacy for a full-time disability insurance position.

QUALIFICATIONS

A medical degree is required for medical director positions in disability insurance. Board certification and an active state license are needed for many roles. Training in musculoskeletal-related specialties, such as orthopedics, occupational medicine, pain management, neurology, physical medicine and rehabilitation, or trauma care, may be desired.

Experience in managed care and utilization review is beneficial.

Involvement in or certification by the American Academy of Insurance Medicine (AAIM) can strengthen an application.

COMPENSATION

Due to the medical decision-making required by disability insurance medical directors, compensation is similar to that of clinical work.

Disability Insurance Medical Director

28. Physician Recruitment and Leadership Consulting

The field of recruitment, executive searches, and staffing is fast-paced, dynamic, and competitive. Within the field, physician recruitment is a particularly sought-after niche due to both challenge and reward. On average, a patient care physician in the United States supports over $3 million in direct and indirect economic output per year.[21] However, recruitment can be difficult in the face of a physician shortage. As a result, organizations seeking to hire physicians are willing to expend resources to do so.

Organizations use in-house physician recruiters or hire external recruitment agencies. In either case, the recruiter is a crucial link between a company and a candidate.

"Recruit to retain" is a mantra in the field, because hiring costs—including recruiting efforts, sign-on bonuses, relocation packages, and new employee training—are high. A physician vacancy is expensive as well, given the resulting gaps in patient care, interrupted workflow, and impact on staff morale.

Executive search firms commonly are asked by clients for services in addition to traditional recruitment. These include leadership consulting, which employers may request to ensure that new organizational leaders will be successful. Consequently, offering another line of business that addresses the "retain" aspect of "recruit to retain" is becoming popular among search firms.

THE ROLE OF NONCLINICAL PHYSICIANS

It is rare to encounter a recruiter who is also a physician, yet physicians are ideal recruiters for their peers, for several reasons.

First, industry knowledge is the most important factor to organizations when selecting between physician staffing firms.[22] Physicians can understand hospital staffing needs from firsthand experience. They can offer insight to the employer about what will lead to a successful search—for instance, improvements to malpractice coverage or added benefits, such as loan forgiveness programs.

Just as they understand the industry and employer needs, physicians can accurately describe the role they are working to fill. Perhaps you've spoken to recruiters who don't seem to have a grasp of the vacancies they're trying to fill. Physicians can effectively sell a position on its strong points. They can explain complex compensation plans and job nuances.

Physicians have sizeable professional networks even before they enter recruiting. They can form new connections with other doctors more easily than recruiters without a clinical background.

Finally, having worked in the field for which they're recruiting, physicians can assist organizations in using innovative recruitment strategies, such as buying small physician practices, retraining physicians who have been out of practice for a period, or recruiting residents early in their training.

Adoption of leadership consulting as a line of business by executive staffing firms was born out of the recognition that a business's success depends on strong leadership. Physicians with leadership experience are in an exceptional position to assist health care organizations in building engaged and adaptable health care leaders.

Employers
- Executive search firm
- Hospital or health care system
- Leadership or organizational consulting firm
- Physician staffing agency

JOB SUMMARY—PHYSICIAN RECRUITER

Similar Job Titles
- Director of Physician Recruitment
- Health Care Recruiter

- Placement Specialist
- Search Consultant

When used effectively, search firms don't just recruit, they provide a spectrum of services. A physician recruiter begins the process of filling an open position by working with the hiring organization to establish their needs and priorities, and then develops a strategy for the search.

Then the recruiter, along with support staff, identifies candidates. This is accomplished using marketing strategies, such as job listings and advertisements, as well as proactively searching sources, such as the firm's database and professional association rosters. The recruiter screens potential candidates, reviews resumes and application materials, and presents the most qualified candidates to the client. To varying degrees, a recruiter may be involved in negotiations after an offer is made.

The job also entails strategic planning for the firm as well as attending conferences and networking events to increase company visibility and build relationships with potential candidates.

Example Responsibilities
- Manage the recruitment life cycle from candidate sourcing to closing vacant positions
- Gather information to understand an organization's physician staffing needs
- Develop and implement recruitment strategies
- Design and manage physician recruitment and placement activities
- Develop relationships with training programs and professional organizations
- Work with organizational leadership to manage staffing needs and reach business growth goals
- Lead recruitment efforts, such as trade show and conference presence

Physician recruiters working in-house for a hospital or other health care organization have similar responsibilities to search firm recruiters, although they may have broader talent acquisition accountability. This can include aligning recruitment efforts with the hospital's credentialing and onboarding activities, developing strategies for provider retention, and contributing to organization-wide changes, such as restructuring and physician practice acquisitions. They may work with external search firms for certain high-level positions or vacancies that are difficult to fill.

OTHER NONCLINICAL JOB OPTIONS

Leadership consultants provide resources, processes, and training to help senior-level staff effectively lead their organizations. Ideally, they do so in a way that allows for measurable results demonstrating individual growth and improvement at the department and organizational level. In addition to working with specific executives, they may be involved in departmental or functional group workshops and overall leadership strategy.

QUALIFICATIONS

Most physician recruiter positions require a bachelor's degree and lower-level recruiting experience. For physicians pursing this line of work, network size and leadership experience weigh more heavily than clinical experience.

COMPENSATION

Recruiter compensation includes a base salary plus a commission for filled positions. Average physician recruiter salaries don't reach six figures. However, average figures are for average recruiters. Given the strengths that a medical degree can bring and the potential for a high success rate in filling vacancies, the opportunity exists to earn a respectable income.

Recruitment and leadership consulting firms are structured similarly to other types of consulting companies, in that consultants can work their way up a defined hierarchy, such as from associate to principal to managing director, with considerable increases in compensation along the way.

Physician Recruiter

Aditi Mallick, MD

JOB TITLE: Engagement Manager

EMPLOYER: McKinsey & Company

What does your organization do?

McKinsey & Company is a global management consulting firm that serves organizations across the private, public, and social sectors to identify and set the direction toward their most important goals and to work with them to turn these ambitious goals into reality.

What is your role within the organization?

Engagement managers lead the execution of a client project while guiding and developing individual team members. I am the main day-to-day contact for clients and take ownership of the overall project and its end products.

What are your responsibilities?

I form the bridge between the project working team, clients, and senior leadership from McKinsey. I lead project teams of analysts and associates through the analysis and design of organizational performance approaches, develop tailor-made solutions alongside our clients, and work closely with clients to ensure sustainable results.

Client project work typically includes gathering and analyzing information, formulating and testing hypotheses, and developing recommendations for presentations to client management. It often includes helping to implement those recommendations with client team members. In addition to the client project work, a major element of the role is to train and develop the colleagues on my teams.

What does a typical day on the job look like?

How I spend my days depends on many factors, including the location and nature of my current project (including whether it's an out-of-town project versus a local project), the client, and my team. That said, there are some common elements. A typical project is 8 to 12 weeks in duration. The consulting team is made up of an engagement manager plus anywhere from two to five analysts and associates divided into different workstreams.

As an engagement manager, I check in with my team around 9 in the morning about what each person is working on and what their schedule for the day is. They might, for example, be developing an approach to deconstructing and solving a problem, performing new analyses, conducting expert interviews, or creating client presentation materials.

I make sure that my colleagues and I are clear on our goals for the day before we launch into our individual work.

Between 9 and 6 o'clock, the day is a mix of interviews (both internal and external), client meetings, team problem-solving sessions, and individual work time. In team problem-solving sessions, we come together as a broader McKinsey team to review progress, refine our insights, and shape how we want to present our findings to our clients. Around 6, we check out as a team, reviewing what, if any, outstanding work remains for the evening. Then we all head our separate ways, which is typically either back to our respective hotels if it's an out-of-town project or home if it's a local project.

How does your medical background and experience contribute to your work?

I do all my work in health care across the private, public, and social sectors, so being a board-certified and practicing physician allows me to bring a unique perspective to my teams and to clients. The impact of my medical background on my work as a consultant crosses four big areas. First, it provides me with a scientific understanding of the basis of disease and therapy, including the scientific method for problem solving. Second, it imparts a deep, real-world appreciation for the clinical context of decisions that comes from maintaining a clinical practice. Third, it gives me a pragmatic view of the health care ecosystem, both from education and from practicing in diverse care settings. Finally, it has given me experience in and a passion for teaching, coaching, and mentoring others.

What are the best parts of your job?

There are three things: the issues I get to work on; the opportunities for professional development; and the people I get to work with.

McKinsey affords the opportunity to help some of the best and largest organizations in the world across all sectors and to solve some of their most difficult problems. I find this intellectually exciting and personally fulfilling because of the positive impact we can create.

McKinsey invests heavily in colleagues' professional development through world-class trainings multiple times a year. My colleagues at McKinsey are some of the smartest, kindest, most passionate people I have met.

What are the main challenges you face?

Coming from academic medicine, it took me a few months at the beginning to adjust to the "business" world—specifically a different skill set and different terminology and style of communication. Many skills from medicine are transferrable to consulting, such as empathy, critical thinking, working in teams, hypothesis generation and testing, adaptability, and time management. However, skills such as financial modeling and building formal presentations took some practice.

Similarly, I had to learn new terms, such as EBITDA (which stands for earnings before interest, tax, depreciation, and amortization) and ROIC (which stands for return on invested capital). Thankfully, McKinsey offers a well-structured crash course called the mini-MBA that blends remote learning with live classroom time to teach non-MBA hires, like MDs, the basics of business.

Where might your career go from here?

This is yet to be determined!

What are some considerations for physicians interested in a career in management consulting?

Strong verbal and written communication are important, including listening, developing a perspective, structuring and organizing around key messages, tailoring to different audiences, and speaking and writing confidently and persuasively.

Management consultants need to have the ability and interest to work in teams. This includes working toward a shared goal, identifying and leveraging strengths across a diverse group, being flexible, supporting and mentoring teammates, treating colleagues with respect, and developing close collaborative relationships with colleagues.

Leadership experience also is valuable. It helps to be able to take responsibility for outcomes, motivate people, give and receive feedback, delegate, train others, and confidently make decisions. Along these lines, empathy, active listening, tact, and diplomacy are beneficial.

Consultants must have time management skills and must be able to set priorities and meet deadlines. They also must take initiative by coming up with ideas and solutions to problems and dealing positively with the unexpected occurrences and challenges.

I recommend speaking to physicians who are consultants to understand the diversity of pathways within consulting. For some people, myself included, it is possible to maintain a clinical practice as a consultant if that is of interest.

Writing and Communications

The term *medical writing* is used to describe any written medical or health content, encompassing a range of material from scientific publications to patient-oriented health articles. In addition to long-form published material, it includes text to accompany visuals, scripts for video and audio content, and technical documents.

The audience varies, as well. Medical writing can be geared toward medical professionals, students, regulatory bodies, patients, or the lay public.

Jobs for physicians in medical writing involve more than actual writing. Physicians are involved in project oversight, conceptualization, and providing medical input to a team of writers.

Medical writing is an attractive career for physicians seeking flexibility and autonomy in their work. It tends to be accompanied by lower stress and less risk than both clinical medicine and other types of nonclinical work.

29. Medical Communications

TV ads and drug rep visits are a small component of marketing and education in the pharmaceutical industry. Print and Web-based informational materials, medical publications, having a presence at scientific meetings, and disease awareness programs are only a few other strategies. Drug companies vary as to how much of this work is done in-house; however, it is common for them to hire medical communications agencies (colloquially referred to as *medcoms*) for some or all of it.

Medical communications agencies provide services to assist pharmaceutical and medical product companies in the communication of scientific data and medical information to a variety of audiences. In addition to producing written material, they offer strategic guidance and planning for publications and educational programs.

A medical writer working within medical education or marketing at a pharmaceutical company is likely to focus on a single therapeutic area or drug class. Most medical communications staff, on the other hand, have a more varied role, focusing on diverse topics and clients. Nonetheless, some companies within the medical communications industry specialize in a particular area, such as continuing medical education or digital media.

THE ROLE OF NONCLINICAL PHYSICIANS

A physician's medical background is valuable in accurately and directly presenting medical information while simultaneously supporting the client's brand and needs. Familiarity with medicine and public health assists in crafting documents that tell a compelling story to stakeholders, such as clinicians or patients.

Medical communications requires a solid understanding of the topic being communicated. This can include disease pathophysiology, drug mechanisms of action, and current treatment guidelines, for instance. As a result, medical communications agencies rely on the help of contracted or employed medical experts to produce scientifically sound content.

As clients look to medical communications companies for more than just written products, knowledge of medicine and clinical practice patterns is valuable in developing publication and educational strategies that will reach the intended audience and be well received.

Employers

- Medical communications agency
- Pharmaceutical company

JOB SUMMARY—MEDICAL COMMUNICATIONS MEDICAL DIRECTOR

Similar Job Titles

- Chief Clinical Officer
- Director of Medical Writing
- Director of Publications and Scientific Content
- Director of Scientific Strategy
- Publications Planning Director
- Scientific Affairs Director
- Strategic Medical Director

A medical communications medical director is responsible for conceptualizing and overseeing deliverable development. Such development might include slide decks for continuing education sessions, reports summarizing advisory board meetings, scripts for educational videos, website copy for advocacy groups, and informational pamphlets.

Projects begin by working with the client company to set project goals, scope, timeframe, and budget. The agency then develops an internal plan to produce the required deliverables. They might recruit freelance writers and scientific experts, depending on their internal capabilities. Next steps include background research, content writing, formatting and developing visuals, and other tasks as required by the project. Following review and approval by the client, the product is delivered and the project closed out.

The extent to which the medical director is responsible for the actual writing of content is variable, depending on company size and project type. Some directors may have the help of a team of medical writers. Conversely, the director at a small firm may spend significant time writing, as well as editing, fact-checking, and reviewing.

With pharmaceutical companies as clients, work can be fast-paced, and needs can change quickly. Medical directors must juggle multiple projects simultaneously and reprioritize work as client needs change. It is not unheard of to work zealously on a project, only for it to be halted when an experimental drug doesn't perform as expected in clinical trials.

Medical directors need to use a critical eye to ensure that written material is medically correct and that any claims made are backed by the client's data from clinical trials and other sources. In some cases, deliverables also must meet restrictions placed on pharmaceutical company publications by regulatory bodies.

Example Responsibilities

- Write and edit materials about a drug or other medical product for a specified audience
- Translate medical and scientific concepts into compelling and digestible language
- Research and identify references to support the claims made in written deliverables
- Build a scientific story that is medically accurate and supports a brand strategy
- Distill large amounts of scientific data into succinct messages
- Identify important information and weave it into publications that drive audience interest
- Work with designers to develop a visual style that is consistent with written material
- Recruit external medical experts to assist with content generation

OTHER NONCLINICAL JOB OPTIONS

Medical writer positions, although they tend to pay less than director roles, can be rewarding, low stress, and make good use of a physician's medical background. Scientific Writer, Promotional Medical Writer, and Medical Marketing Writer are similar job titles.

QUALIFICATIONS

Few medical communications positions require a medical degree, although many agencies prefer an MD or other advanced scientific degree for director-level staff. Even if not required, an advanced degree can provide a leg up in getting hired and subsequently promoted.

Neither board certification nor clinical experience usually is required, but both may be helpful in securing positions within a therapeutic area that aligns with a candidate's training or experience.

Scientific writing experience often is required. Some employers will request a list of the applicant's publications. They'll want to see evidence that a candidate is able to generate succinct, comprehensible messages from complex data or technical information.

Across the broad field of medical writing, medical communications is a good choice for a physician who works well under pressure and with a deadline in place.

COMPENSATION

Salaries for physicians in medical communications tend to be on the low side, but frequently surpass six figures. Employees with a doctorate can earn more than those without, although increased compensation is generally accompanied by a higher responsibility level, management duties, and client interactions.

Medical Communications Medical Director

Medical Writer

30. Medical Journalism

Journalism is not dying. It is merely changing. The general public has easy access to erroneous, negative, and downright false information in mobile and online formats. And the majority of the public gets most of their information about science from the mass media.[23] Journalistic excellence is more important now than ever.

Medical journalism combines the science of medicine and the art of journalism. This results in a unique field that blends the dissemination of medical information with aspects of creativity and critical analysis. A great deal of medical journalism aims to bridge a gap between researchers and consumers.

Medical journalism is distinct from other types of journalism in that it conveys medical material, including highly technical and scientific information that requires accurate interpretation by the writer. Precise summarization, statistical reporting, and communication about medically related problems are necessary to ensure a quality and reputable product.

News pieces, investigative reporting, feature writing, and columns are all forms of medical journalism. Broadly speaking, *news* is information transmitted from a source to an audience through a journalist. It focuses on events and issues in a straightforward, unbiased manner. The intended audience for an article greatly influences the content, writing style, and depth of information presented.

THE ROLE OF NONCLINICAL PHYSICIANS

A comprehension of medical topics is what sets a medical journalist apart from journalists as a whole. In conjunction with having a grasp of the science and medicine, physicians have a comprehensive understanding of how scientists and doctors think, how to translate industry jargon into simple English, and how to communicate medical information in a compelling manner.

Specialized, in-depth reporting on a particular sector or issue is called *beat reporting,* and it tends to be the bread and butter for physicians in journalism. Medical, health, and science beat reporting is common in newspapers, magazines, and other media outlets.

Journalists are, in a sense, gatekeepers. Physicians working as medical journalists can assist in curbing claims of sensationalism and biased reporting in the media by using their medical experience to provide truthful and elucidative accounts.

Employers
- Magazine or other publisher
- News media network
- Nontraditional media outlet, such as an Internet publisher

JOB SUMMARY—MEDICAL JOURNALIST

Similar Job Titles
- Health Journalist
- Managing Editor
- Medical Writer
- Research Journalist
- Science Writer
- Science Writing Associate

Medical journalists plan, analyze, write, and edit articles on topics related to medicine and current health care affairs. Reports are used for publication in both print and electronic media. Some are broadcast on television or other outlets.

Journalists work closely with a news team consisting of other journalists, reporters, editors, graphic designers, and photographers. As a topic expert, a physician in this role may be primarily responsible for reviewing and editing the content initially developed by another journalist.

As with clinical medicine, ethics often must be considered in medical journalism. Author misconduct, plagiarism, data fabrication, "lack of knowledge" leading to false reporting, and conflicts of interest all come into play. Medical journalists expend significant effort in considering different sides of an issue, determining how to put stories into context, and exploring angles that may affect the overall feel or voice of a piece.

Example Responsibilities

- Interview medical professionals, patients, and organization representatives
- Attend meetings, events, and conferences to cover medical updates and policy changes
- Identify areas of need and gaps in available content on a topic
- Gather, evaluate, and interpret complex information
- Provide analytical content about current health and medical events and topics
- Conduct research using various sources to derive data and facts for use in articles

QUALIFICATIONS

Medical journalism doesn't require a medical degree or certification. Nonetheless, an MD provides immediate legitimacy and can help in getting your foot in the door with a desirable organization. It also can assist in being assigned to particularly interesting or high-profile assignments.

Strong writing skills and previous publications are needed for landing most jobs in the field. However, experience is not necessarily more important than ability and skill. Medical journalists must be able to critically evaluate evidence and rapidly develop engaging pieces. They must have a natural interest in current events.

COMPENSATION

Compensation for employed science journalism jobs is significantly less than that of clinical jobs. Physicians with an aptitude and passion for journalism can progress to writing for prestigious publications, work their way up in an organization, or become well-known authors.

Journalism depends on timely reporting. Consequently, certain roles require an irregular schedule. Hours can be long in the case of a noteworthy or developing event. On the other hand, longer-term investigative work and articles written for less frequently published outlets offer a less taxing schedule.

Medical Journalist

31. Medical Publishing

"Publish or perish" is a phrase you have probably heard if you've spent any time in an academic setting. Scientific publishing is one of the primary avenues to spread knowledge within the medical field. Physicians who publish their research are rewarded with the satisfaction of knowing they've made an intellectual contribution to science. Doctors can, in fact, turn this satisfaction into a career.

Scholarly work in medicine is published in several formats, including books, journals, and online. Whatever the publisher's preferred format and focus area, it relies on staff with strong scientific backgrounds to effectively propagate new knowledge and ideas.

Both challenges and opportunities exist in publishing. Clinicians and scientists often are overwhelmed by the volume of information available to them, yet find it difficult to locate the material they need. The rapid rate at which medical information and data are generated makes it difficult to ensure that material is published in a timely and accessible manner while simultaneously ensuring quality.

Traditional books and journals are no longer the best way to disseminate certain scientific and medical information. Innovation in medical publishing includes open source material, interactive databases, central repositories, and the use of machine intelligence to address difficulties such as publication bias and inappropriate categorization.

Publications geared toward a patient audience include patient education websites, pamphlets, and other consumer-oriented information. A 1959 article on the topic of health education noted: "So far, at least, we seem to have failed to impress all or most individuals with the importance of achieving and maintaining their own bodily health."[24] Now, six decades later, we are in a similar position, but with more outlets to educate patients, improved methods to drive messages to the right populations, a better understanding of human behavior and decision making, and new technologies to assist.

THE ROLE OF NONCLINICAL PHYSICIANS

As clinicians, we are taught to practice evidence-based medicine. Medical publishing is a key component of getting evidence into practice. Physicians are equipped to ensure that the transition and incorporation of evidence is successful. Just as, in medicine, we aim to deliver the right care to the right patient at the right time, in publishing there is a need to deliver the right information to the right audience in the right format at the right time.

Most physicians have, at some point in their careers, published their research results. Many have volunteered their time as a journal peer reviewer. Familiarity with the processes of manuscript writing, journal selection, submission, and review is valuable for a medical publishing role.

Employers
- Academic publisher
- Alternative media company, such as a point-of-care medical reference
- Medical journal
- Online or electronic media publisher
- University press

JOB SUMMARY—EDITOR-IN-CHIEF

Similar Job Titles
- Editorial Board Chairman
- Editorial Director
- Managing Editor
- Medical Editor
- Scientific Publication Director

The medical publishing job most identifiable to medical professionals is that of medical journal editor. This and other careers for physicians in medical publishing involve more than the actual act of writing. They incorporate editing, planning, fact-checking, production management, and marketing.

A journal editor-in-chief is responsible for planning each journal issue and making final decisions about manuscript inclusion. The editor develops the overall journal strategy, ensuring that the content fits with the publication's mission and with trends in the field.

Primary research articles make up only a portion of a journal. Reviews, opinions, letters, and essays are included as well. The editor oversees this mix and finds a suitable balance based on the journal's readership and goals.

Leading outreach and networking efforts in the scientific community to promote the journal and recruit submissions is another important part of the job.

The editor identifies trends in research, staying abreast of relevant literature and keeping up with developments in methodologies. Journal editors must strategize to sustain the journal's quality and reputation as the medical field progresses.

Example Responsibilities

- Collate information about a medical topic area from a variety of sources
- Evaluate submitted manuscripts and prepare them for production
- Review the impact and effectiveness of published materials
- Identify clinical relevance of manuscripts and articles
- Commission contributions from respected medical community researchers and leaders
- Represent the publisher at conferences and meetings, fostering partnerships and acting as an ambassador

OTHER NONCLINICAL JOB OPTIONS

Newer medical publishing formats, such as those that are exclusively online, embrace medicine's rapidly evolving evidence base. Web-based point-of-care reference tools fall into this category and represent another career option for physicians in medical publishing. These companies rely heavily on physicians to contribute to and critically revise their publications.

QUALIFICATIONS

Like other medical writing careers, medical publishing doesn't require residency training or a medical license. Senior positions, such as medical journal editor-in-chief, however, may require extensive experience in the publication's specialty area.

A background in research and authoring scientific journal articles is beneficial. Success in medical publishing depends on ongoing curiosity and the ability to think conceptually about a range of scientific issues.

COMPENSATION

Compensation in medical publishing is not stellar. Even chief editors of top journals earn less than physicians in clinical practice. As with other careers in medical writing, though, the low risk, reasonable workload, and flexible schedule can make it worthwhile.

Physicians can earn more than those without a doctoral degree in medical publishing; however, their position often is accompanied by leadership and management responsibilities.

Editor-in-Chief

Medical Education Content Development and Test Prep

Mastery of the minimum necessary knowledge to practice medicine is a huge undertaking. The volume of material that medical students and trainees must learn is immense and continues to grow. Medical education is no longer limited to classroom lectures, textbooks, and bedside teaching. Students now rely on extensive review materials, Web-based resources, and self-paced and adaptive curricula to digest information efficiently.

The need for innovation in medical education extends past four years of medical school. A career in medicine is a commitment to lifelong learning. To keep up with advances in medicine requires consistently learning new material, which must be squeezed in with our already hectic schedules.

Educational content offered outside of academia by for-profit companies has become progressively common and high quality, and is increasingly recognized for playing a crucial role in all learning stages for medical professionals.

Test preparation is a noteworthy component of this industry. Having prevailed through medical school and the USMLE, you're aware of the test prep industry's significance in medicine. High-stakes, standardized tests also are prevalent in other health professions, including nursing, physician assisting, pharmacy, and therapy.

Trends in the test prep field include use of augmented reality, gamification, and techniques to enhance a learner's overall experience by telling a story or otherwise creating memorable encounters with the material.

THE ROLE OF NONCLINICAL PHYSICIANS

Physicians can provide clinical insight within medical education companies on a high level as well as work in the trenches on content development. Organizations benefit from physician-level mastery of medical concepts to create effective material that is competitive in the marketplace.

Employers

- Continuing professional education provider
- Educational institution
- E-learning provider
- Medical test prep company

JOB SUMMARY—MEDICAL EDUCATION CONTENT CREATOR

Similar Job Titles

- Clinical Content Editor
- Educational Content Developer
- Item Writer
- Medical Writer
- Physician Author

A medical education content creator turns complex scientific facts into consumable information that will spark the learner's interest and retain their attention. Depending on the company, the job may be aimed at supporting medical student and trainee learning, preparing health sciences professionals to pass required exams, or keeping physicians current on evidence-based and emerging medical topics within their specialties.

A content creator's job involves writing summaries or explanations of medical concepts, fact and data checking, and reviewing previously written material for ongoing relevance and accuracy. Positions with test prep companies often involve an element of question writing (referred to in the industry as *item writing*), including patient case vignettes and clinical scenarios.

When the subject matter is new to the content creator, this job can require in-depth subject research and background learning in order to synthesize information for the intended audience. Test prep products in highly specialized topic areas can require content creators to recruit and contract with external experts.

In addition to staying updated on medical and clinical information, content creators must stay informed of changes to certifying organizations' test formats and blueprints.

Example Responsibilities
- Review and edit content for quality and consistency
- Explain complex clinical concepts and disease processes in written format
- Revise previously developed content to ensure relevance and ongoing accuracy
- Write basic medical and clinical assessment items and corresponding explanations
- Identify topics for new material development
- Work with illustrators and graphic designers to visually portray concepts
- Evaluate product metrics and work to improve product workflows and formats

OTHER NONCLINICAL JOB OPTIONS

Given their backgrounds, physicians in medical education content development often take on a leadership or subject matter expert role, working with or overseeing a team of writers and editors. These positions include Director of Curriculum Development, Director of Medical Content Development, and Medical Director.

A design career in the medical content and test prep space can be fitting for creative and artistic physicians. Job titles include Medical Illustrator, Creative Director, and Medical Media Specialist. These roles are focused on providing visual content in the form of digital images, animations, videos, and other multimedia to enhance or clarify written material.

QUALIFICATIONS

Any experience level can land you a job in content development. The format and topic of the content being developed determines the need for specialty training and other requirements. Content development and test prep can be a fitting field for early-career physicians interested in medical writing. The less removed a writer is from learning the material or taking the tests, the more that physician can empathize with customers' learning needs.

Companies hiring for a position that doesn't require a medical degree may have a preference for an advanced degree in a health or sciences field, making physicians strong candidates.

Applicants may be asked to demonstrate their writing ability. Test prep companies may require candidates to have achieved certain scores on medical exams.

COMPENSATION

As with other full-time jobs in medical writing and communications, compensation often doesn't compete with that for clinical work. Salaries depend on the content type and the extent to which it relies on the writer's medical expertise.

Medical Education Content Creator

Medical Illustrator

Dragon Do, MD

JOB TITLE: Content Developer

EMPLOYER: A medium-sized company focused on creating practice questions for standardized exams

What does your organization do?

My company is focused on creating the highest quality educational products for standardized exams, including USMLE, MCAT, NCLEX, SAT, and ACT. This is accomplished primarily through practice test questions. They have a large emphasis on medical and health professional exams.

What is your role within the organization?

I am part of the company's Medical Content Development team. I focus on writing and reviewing questions for USMLE practice question banks.

What are your responsibilities?

I work in a team of physician authors. We review medical topics that are tested on USMLE Steps 1, 2, and 3. I write questions to teach specific educational objectives related to the various topics. I also review existing questions from our question bank and edit them as needed.

What does a typical day on the job look like?

I get to the office around 8 o'clock. I grab some coffee and head to my desk. I then check my email, calendar, and notes to plan out my day. I usually already have a set of four to five questions in my work queue that I had started working on a couple days earlier. The questions usually revolve around a specific clinical topic. I go through each question, tweaking the question stem, playing around with wrong answer options, or reading articles related to the clinical topic. Most of the time I am thinking and writing.

I work at my own pace but do have occasional meetings with my team to go over questions. We review each other's questions and discuss how to refine them. Sometimes during these sessions I realize I must totally revamp a question.

I usually take a break for lunch midday and then return to continue writing. Sometimes I may talk to the other physicians about interesting cases. When a question is ready, I send it to my colleagues for a more formal review. Some questions may come back to me if they need adjusting. I leave the office around 4:30. My work hours are flexible, and I can shift them to be earlier or later as long as I get the work done.

How does your medical background and experience contribute to your work?

I completed a fellowship in pediatric hematology-oncology after my general pediatrics residency. With my training background, the questions I focus on in our question banks tend to be related to pediatrics or hematology-oncology. My clinical experiences provide ideas to help me craft questions that are realistic and unique. My hematology-oncology background, along with having done some basic science research in a bench lab during fellowship, helps me think through various question subtleties to make scenarios interesting.

What are the best parts of your job?

During fellowship, I realized the aspect I enjoyed most about being a physician was the educational opportunity. I found it rewarding when I was able to empower a parent or medical trainee to take care of the patient. I accomplished this through various teaching avenues, including writing. I always felt a degree of satisfaction when I was able to put together a well-written and useful medical consult note.

Although I liked clinical work, treating young oncology patients provided me a unique perspective on the importance of quality time with loved ones. Work–life balance became a priority for me. I like that I can continue teaching without having the super-busy lifestyle of a full-time clinician. In addition to the work–life balance and teaching focus, I value being able to work in the background and pace myself accordingly.

What are the main challenges you face?

It can take lot of time to craft high-quality questions for some educational topics. A question may need to be revised or rewritten several times before it is ready to be used.

Where might your career go from here?

I hope to continue writing and working in medical education.

What are some considerations for physicians interested in a career in medical writing?

Enjoyment of reading, thinking, and writing lend themselves to a career in medical education content development. Grammar skills are vital, as well. I spend significant time adjusting the details of a question stem and reworking the stem and answer choices.

Physicians in medical writing positions are both teachers and learners. An interest in teaching medical topics and an understanding of strategies for how to best convey the information is important. You need to stay up to date with new advances in medicine, so an interest in ongoing learning about all aspects of medicine is useful.

Depending on the specific company or product area, having previously performed well in relevant courses or on standardized tests is necessary. In my position, for example, a solid understanding of concepts covered on the USMLE helps with understanding the material in order to write relevant test prep questions and explanations. A lot goes into developing a quality, accurate, and fair test question.

Although medical writing seems like an independent job on the surface, it really is team oriented. Physicians in this field need to be team players. It is important to keep the goals of the company or project in mind and not take criticism too personally.

Public Health and Government

Public health is the science of promoting health, preventing disease, and prolonging life through methodized efforts of organizations, communities, and individuals. Whereas clinical medicine is patient-focused and centered around diagnosis and treatment, public health is population-focused and more heavily concentrated on prevention and overall health.

U.S. public health achievements in the last several decades include:

- Prevention of infectious diseases through improved vaccination
- Improved motor vehicle safety
- Safer workplaces
- Decline in death rates from cardiovascular disease
- Improvements to maternal and child health
- Improved food safety
- Reduction in tobacco use

Jobs in public health allow physicians to make a difference in the health of an entire community or to impact the policies that affect our population as a whole.

U.S. Health and Human Services

The federal government employs more people than any single company in the United States. Because maintaining the population's health is a key role of the government, a significant percentage of governmental positions are related to health and medicine. The Department of Health and Human Services (HHS) employs most physician government workers. The positions and responsibilities within HHS, though, are wide-ranging, due to the variety of agencies and divisions that make up HHS.

Many HHS jobs that are suitable for physicians are similar in focus to private sector nonclinical jobs and nongovernmental public health jobs. Consequently, there is some overlap between the careers profiled here and those in other chapters. Federal government jobs, however, are somewhat distinct in their funding, oversight, and bureaucracy, so they are reviewed separately.

THE ROLE OF NONCLINICAL PHYSICIANS

All physicians working for HHS assist the department in improving the health and wellbeing of the country.

A predominant job for nonclinical physicians across HHS agencies is that of a medical officer. In many ways, this title is analogous to the role of a medical director in the private sector. The focal areas and responsibilities can vary considerably between medical officers, as they can for medical directors. What physicians in these positions have in common is that they serve as advisors, administrators, and consultants, using their medical knowledge and experience to assist in carrying out the organization's mission and strategic priorities.

Employers
- Centers for Disease Control and Prevention (CDC)
- Centers for Medicare & Medicaid Services (CMS)

- FDA
- National Institutes of Health (NIH)

Similar Job Titles

- Division Chief or Director
- Medical Officer
- Medical Research Scientist
- Scientific Officer
- Senior Advisor
- Supervisory Physician

JOBS WITH THE CENTERS FOR DISEASE CONTROL AND PREVENTION

Thanks to the media, hearing "CDC" tends to conjure mental images of workers in hazmat suits clustered around a gurney. Disease outbreak investigation and response is certainly an important part of what the CDC does, although the agency's reach surpasses this. As the leading U.S. public health institute, the CDC aims to protect the public's health by disease prevention and control in a number of areas, including infectious disease, environmental health, occupational health and safety, and foodborne illness.

Several approaches are used in the CDC's work, including response to health threats and outbreaks, disease surveillance, scientific research, information distribution, and health promotion initiatives.

The CDC's efforts extend beyond U.S. borders in an effort to make progress against disease epidemics worldwide. Both United States–based employees and staff in over 50 countries are involved in international projects.

Divisions within the CDC that are popular for medical professionals include the following:

- Center for Global Health
- National Institute for Occupational Safety and Health (NIOSH)
- Office of Noncommunicable Disease, Injury, and Environmental Health
- Office of Public Health Preparedness and Response

CDC medical officers are responsible for leading a center's strategic priority efforts or overseeing implementation of major initiatives.

Example Responsibilities

- Evaluate medical research and identify causes or sources of diseases and outbreaks
- Apply epidemiologic principles to investigate and analyze disease-related problems
- Make recommendations for procedures to control disease
- Streamline public health processes, procedures, and knowledge bases
- Provide medical advice and consultation on critical public health issues

Physicians for whom a career with the CDC sounds interesting may want to consider positions with HHS's Office of Global Affairs (OGA) or Health Resources Services Administration (HRSA).

JOBS WITH THE FOOD AND DRUG ADMINISTRATION

Whereas the CDC conducts health promotion and prevention activities, the FDA regulates and enforces standards affecting the population's health.

The FDA is tasked with ensuring the efficacy, safety, and security of drugs, medical devices, biologics, food, cosmetics, and radiation-emitting products. Notably, about 20 cents of every dollar spent by consumers in the United States is spent on products regulated by the FDA.[25]

In addition to reviewing and approving submissions for new products, the FDA conducts ongoing surveillance of products already on the market and supports innovative medical products in reaching the public. Additionally, the FDA regulates tobacco products and plays a significant role in the ability of the United States to address terrorism through medical countermeasures.

Doctors transitioning to a nonclinical job with the FDA may appreciate the opportunity to conduct risk-versus-benefit analyses similar to those used in patient care, but with an entire population in mind.

Physicians are everywhere within the FDA. These are just a handful of agency divisions that hire nonclinical physicians:

- Center for Biologics Evaluation and Research
- Center for Devices and Radiological Health
- Center for Drug Evaluation and Research
- Office of Health Informatics
- Office of Policy, Planning, Legislation, and Analysis

A customary initial role for a physician with the FDA is that of a clinical reviewer. This job involves reviewing submissions from biopharmaceutical companies, which can take place prior to, during, and after a company conducts clinical trials. Reviewers meet with drug company staff throughout the process to provide guidance and make recommendations. Physician reviewers work closely with statisticians, pharmacologists, biologists, and administrative staff to comprehensively analyze documents.

Example Responsibilities
- Determine drug and medical product efficacy and safety based on scientific and clinical data
- Provide advice and technical expertise in a clinical or therapeutic area
- Monitor safety and effectiveness of medical products currently on the market
- Establish policies regarding medical product data analysis and interpretation

The Substance Abuse and Mental Health Services Administration (SAMHSA) and the Office of the National Coordinator for Health Information Technology (ONC) are other options within HHS for physicians intrigued by career opportunities with the FDA. Physicians interested in work related to nutrition and food can consider jobs with the U.S. Department of Agriculture, such as in the Center for Nutrition Policy and Promotion.

JOBS WITH THE CENTERS FOR MEDICARE & MEDICAID SERVICES

Physician careers with CMS are, loosely speaking, the governmental equivalent of a career in managed care administration.

CMS's mission involves strengthening and modernizing the U.S. health care system while providing quality, cost-effective care. They are a major health care services payer through their own programs—Medicare, Medicaid, and Children's Health Insurance Program (CHIP)—but also influence the broader U.S. health care marketplace.

A few CMS divisions that employ medical professionals are:

- Center for Medicaid and CHIP Services
- Office of Minority Health
- The CMS Innovation Center

The CMS Innovation Center, which was established in 2010 as a result of the Affordable Care Act, tests innovative payment and delivery system models to tie health care reimbursement to better outcomes, making it a noteworthy career option for physicians.

Example Responsibilities

- Evaluate the effectiveness of existing payment models
- Serve as an advisor in the design and implementation of new payment models and initiatives
- Review proposed policy changes and their potential impact on patients covered by Medicare and Medicaid
- Engage with medical providers regarding CMS's goals and disseminate national health care strategies
- Analyze data to inform decisions about reimbursement
- Test new payment and delivery models to improve care and lower costs
- Recommend legislative actions to improve health care delivery and reimbursement

Other HHS options have some overlap with responsibilities of a CMS physician. The Office of Disease Prevention and Health Promotion develops national health goals and programs, including the Healthy People objectives. The Agency for Health Care Research and Quality invests in research and training related to the U.S. health care delivery system, with its work often informing decisions made by CMS.

JOBS WITH THE NATIONAL INSTITUTES OF HEALTH

The NIH focuses heavily on scientific research, in contrast to other HHS agencies that concentrate on programs, services, and regulation.

The NIH's mission is to seek knowledge about the nature and behavior of living systems and the application of that knowledge to reduce illness and enhance health. To accomplish this, they conduct their own research internally, as well as provide research funding through extramural programs.

NIH divisions and institutes to consider include:

- Biosafety, Biosecurity, and Emerging Biotechnology Policy Division
- Clinical and Healthcare Research Policy Division
- Division of Medical and Clinical Review
- Division of Scientific Programs
- National Cancer Institute
- National Heart, Blood, and Lung Institute

Medical officers at NIH are assigned to a specialty area, and are tasked with planning, implementing, and evaluating programs and initiatives within that area. Not all physician opportunities with NIH are research-based, however. Positions suitable for MDs can focus on tangential areas, such as science policy, education and communication, or technology transfer.

Example Responsibilities
- Develop policy for the conduct of research with human subjects
- Ensure compliance with guidelines and regulation regarding scientific research
- Define research activities and engage collaborators in those activities
- Establish and update human subjects research educational requirements for research staff
- Identify trends and evolving viewpoints in human subjects research
- Provide expert advice and guidance to NIH leadership on complex issues-related research

OTHER FEDERAL GOVERNMENT POSITIONS FOR PHYSICIANS

Federal departments other than HHS hire a limited number of physicians for nonclinical roles. The Occupational Safety and Health Administration (OSHA) and Environmental Protection Agency (EPA), for example, may hire physicians with responsibilities similar to those discussed in the chapter on occupational and environmental health. Physician jobs with the Federal Communications Commission (FCC), the Securities and Exchange Commission (SEC), and other agencies include components of health policy and health IT.

QUALIFICATIONS

Many physicians in HHS have completed a residency and are board-certified, although whether this is required is job-dependent. For instance, cardiology training typically is required for an FDA medical officer who is responsible for reviewing cardiology drug applications.

Given the breadth of federal government jobs for physicians, no single set of skills or attributes is needed. Rather, some backgrounds and strengths are better suited to certain departments. Analytically minded physicians may excel in the FDA, whereas communication skills may be more valuable for certain CDC positions.

Research experience or an MD/PhD dual doctorate are valued for some HHS jobs, such as many within the NIH. Public health knowledge, either through earning an MPH or hands-on experience, is beneficial. The need for clinical experience depends on the position. Involvement in health care administration, health care quality, and public–private partnerships may be useful.

APPLYING TO FEDERAL GOVERNMENT JOBS

The federal government's job application process is different from that of private-sector employers. Applicant requirements can be strict. Most applications are processed through the USAJobs.gov website. Applicant resumes sent through this system must include extensive detail about prior experience and responsibilities. In other cases, vacancies are filled through word of mouth, job fairs, recruiting events, and alternative hiring processes in cases of urgent staffing needs.

CAREER PATHS AND TRAINING

A strength of HHS is the training opportunities it provides for physicians, both on the job and through programs that can lead to full-time employment.

A notable example is the Epidemic Intelligence Service (EIS), a two-year program run through the CDC. EIS fellows begin the program with training in disease surveillance and epidemiology. This is followed by placement at a CDC branch, where they may be involved in field investigations, public health surveillance, epidemiologic analysis, and response to disease outbreaks. EIS alumni are strong candidates for continuing a nonclinical career within or outside of the CDC.

Joining the U.S. Public Health Service Commissioned Corps is another career path option for physicians interested in working for HHS. The Corps is one of the seven uniformed services in the U.S. and is led by the Surgeon General. Members receive the same benefits as members of other uniformed services and, similarly, make a commitment to assist the country in times of need, such as during outbreaks or following natural disasters.

COMPENSATION

HHS salaries are determined by the government's pay scale. The pay often is somewhat lower than similar roles in the private sector.

Although people groan about government jobs, the advantages are undeniable. Federal jobs for physicians boast great benefits, including strong work–life balance, federal holidays, and generous vacation and sick leave policies. Job security is high. Professional development and continuing education are encouraged. There is also opportunity for advancement in an agency or for movement between HHS agencies.

Medical Officer

State and Local Health Department Leadership

The impact of public health efforts on our nation's health is tremendous. Achievements include infectious disease control through vaccination, improved access to safe food and water, reductions in child mortality, and tobacco control, to name a few.

Despite these advances, however, the relevance of local and state public health has increased in recent decades. As we've become better at controlling infectious disease, focus has shifted toward preventing and addressing chronic conditions. What were once considered the medical problems of individuals have become public health emphases. Opioid abuse, vaccine hesitancy, and obesity, in particular, are greatly affecting our communities and our workforces.

State and local health departments have a broad mission—to promote, protect, and improve health. Their priorities will continue to transform as health departments work with federal agencies to respond to climate change, emerging pathogens, and other incipient threats.

THE ROLE OF NONCLINICAL PHYSICIANS

Public health departments depend on physicians in both direct patient care and nonclinical roles. For nonclinical positions, it is depth of scientific knowledge combined with training and experience in multiple health care settings that puts physicians in a prime position to address the far-reaching health needs of a population.

A physician's role in a health department is expansive. This is truly a career for the renaissance physician. The work includes aspects of epidemiology, disease surveillance, health analytics, health policy, and occupational and environmental health.

A health department's success depends, to some extent, on relationships with other organizations within the community. Physicians can forge relationships with local hospitals, medical practices and associations, and nonprofits using a combination of expertise on health issues, personal connections, and the esteem that tends to accompany an MD degree.

Employers
- County, district, or city department of health
- State department of health

JOB SUMMARY—HEALTH OFFICER

Similar Job Titles
- Chief of Medical Services
- Commissioner of Health
- Health Administrator
- Health Director
- Medical Officer
- Medical Program Administrator
- Public Health Officer

A health officer is responsible for overseeing a public health department's services and initiatives. This individual provides leadership and supervision to the department's managers and employees and ensures that the work being conducted is in line with current public health priorities. The health officer is under the direction of a board of health, which provides guidance on these priorities.

Health officers work to assess public health heeds, develop and improve services, and evaluate program effectiveness. This must be done while ensuring legal compliance and alignment with the work of other governmental departments.

Health department structure differs significantly from state to state. Regardless of how the department is organized, the health officer works closely with epidemiologists, biostatisticians, environmentalists, social workers, community health educators, public health nurses, and other physicians.

In a state-level position, the health officer may focus on policy development and continuity with federal and local public health departments via resource linkage. At the district or local level, a bulk of the health officer's time may be spent providing mandated public health services and ensuring that public health codes are addressed.

Although much of a health officer's work involves applying medical expertise to population-level health issues, other aspects are fairly removed from medicine. This includes managing some or all of the department's budget as well as identifying potential funding and revenue sources, such as grants. Ensuring a strong workforce through hiring, training, and promoting organizational culture is an essential part of the job. Political issues inevitably make their way into a health officer's work, as does both wanted and unwanted media attention.

Example Responsibilities

- Meet with the Board of Health to review and discuss priorities
- Interpret and apply policies and laws relating to the department's activities
- Provide guidance and direction to management in all divisions
- Oversee the department's budget and data to justify it
- Develop and implement long- and short-term program objectives
- Communicate with the media about public health threats and department initiatives
- Liaise with the medical community regarding issues that affect overall public health
- Structure partnerships with external organizations

OTHER NONCLINICAL JOB OPTIONS

In states and large district jurisdictions, there are numerous nonclinical jobs for physicians in the department of public health. Often one or more deputy health officers report to the lead health officer. It is common to have a separate physician officer in charge of each of numerous divisions, such as infectious disease control, maternal and child health, environmental health, mental health, and health equity.

QUALIFICATIONS

Postgraduate training is needed for administrative physician positions in health departments. Board certification in public health and preventive medicine is available, although many specialties are fitting and acceptable for work as a health officer, including internal medicine, emergency medicine, infectious disease, and family medicine.

An MPH or other degree in public health provides a great context for the job and may be preferred for candidates.

COMPENSATION

Like other governmental roles, health officer salaries tend to lag behind those of similar private sector jobs. Perks and benefits offset this for some physicians. Local health departments run on normal business hours. Employees enjoy generous time off and retirement benefits.

Between 50 states and over 3000 counties, there are many public health departments across the United States. This can be a plus for physicians needing or wanting to remain in their current geographic location when transitioning to a nonclinical job.

Health Officer

35. Global Health

Global health encompasses practice, research, and study that aims to improve health and achieve health equity for people worldwide.

The United States is motivated to participate in global health efforts to prevent U.S. epidemics, develop international relations, safeguard global commerce, and protect its citizens overseas. In addition to these motives, individuals involved in global health often are driven by humanism and social justice.

Priorities of global health organizations vary. They depend on the major morbidities and mortalities within countries of focus, the characteristics of the populations they serve, and funding sources. What they have in common is a mission to address health needs on a global scale.

Many global health efforts are the same as those being addressed domestically, including mental illness, chronic disease, and violence. However, global solutions to health problems must contend with the unique challenges of international populations. Global health problems often stem from political, environmental, social, and economic issues and inequalities that add complexity.

This field has grown due to an increased recognition of the fundamentally global nature of disease. With this recognition, global health efforts have benefited from increased funding and an expanded use of partnerships across governments and between public and private organizations.

THE ROLE OF NONCLINICAL PHYSICIANS

A global health career for a physician doesn't necessarily require living overseas, participating in relief efforts, or directly caring for underserved populations. Global health organizations are diverse in the services they provide. As a result, global health careers for doctors are similarly varied, with new opportunities being forged as health issues evolve and technological advances alter the way we approach them.

Physicians bring critically needed technical skills to global health organizations, helping to ensure that efforts are medically sound and relevant to the needs of the populations being served. They provide subject matter expertise to disease-specific efforts or to programs geared toward a certain population or geographic area.

Building capacity to meet current and emerging health needs is an important component of many nonclinical jobs in global health, and one in which physicians excel. Global health programs often are implemented with the assistance of an international organization, but aim to train a workforce and build technical and leadership skills that will lead to program sustainability through local resources.

Employers

- Academic institution
- Federal government agency, such as the United States Agency for International Development (USAID)
- International agency, such as WHO
- Medical aid organization
- Nonprofit organization
- Research or consulting firm

JOB SUMMARY—MEDICAL ADVISOR

Similar Job Titles

- Executive Director
- Medical Officer
- Program Director
- Technical Advisor

A medical advisor, such as one employed by WHO, provides both leadership and technical support. WHO is a United Nations agency and a principal global health organization, supporting governments in improving health services for their populations through activities ranging from addressing disease outbreaks to developing best practice guidelines.

A WHO medical advisor has a focal area, such as noncommunicable disease, diarrheal disease, malaria, or HIV/AIDS. This job involves developing and scaling evidence-based strategies, guidelines, and toolkits to assist governments in their approach to the disease area. Detection, prevention, and management efforts may be included. A medical advisor works to identify and incubate new ways to expand or improve efforts.

As with any global health initiatives, many stakeholders are involved. Medical advisors must work closely with division staff, but also coordinate among departments, health areas, and recipient governments.

Example Responsibilities
- Provide medical expertise to program implementation and adaptation
- Expand and sustain country partnerships and mobilize resources
- Support communication strategies for countries developing disease initiatives
- Work with multiple stakeholders to coordinate disease program activities
- Prepare reports and other materials for donors and funders
- Oversee the implementation of plans and programs in participating countries
- Strengthen the capacity of local and regional health workers
- Oversee operational research, surveillance, and health surveys

OTHER NONCLINICAL JOB OPTIONS

Global health positions on the medical advisor level can require considerable experience, sometimes in a specific field or position type. Other roles with less stringent requirements may be of interest to physicians. These include global health researcher, health specialist, and field consultant.

QUALIFICATIONS

The need for specialty training for physicians in global health depends the needs of the organization and the responsibilities of the position. For a role with a specific disease focus, as is the case with most WHO medical advisor positions, either board certification or extensive experience working in a specialty area is highly desirable.

An active medical license typically is not required for nonclinical jobs in global health.

An MPH carries weight for a global health career. Experience in public health program management, epidemiologic analysis, and other public health skills is advantageous.

Some positions require candidates to have lived and worked in a developing country. It can be helpful to be multilingual; however, this rarely is a requirement for nonclinical positions.

COMPENSATION

As with governmental positions, many global health organizations roles have a standard pay system. This may be adjusted for the cost of living at a particular duty station.

The opportunity to travel internationally is a benefit for some physicians pursuing global health careers. For others, it is a barrier. Internationally based physicians may be offered home leave, allowances for dependent family members, and other benefits aimed to lessen the burden of living and working outside the United States.

Global Health Medical Advisor

36. Occupational and Environmental Health

More than 128 million American workers spend an average of 44 hours per week at work.[26,27] For many workers, that time is filled with tasks and exposures that can greatly influence their health. Occupational health and medicine focuses on employee health needs in work settings ranging from factories to offices.

The closely related field of environmental health is focused on preventing and managing adverse health outcomes from exposure to chemical, physical, or biologic agents in either a workplace or the community.

Employers have the responsibility to provide a safe workplace. To do this, they must follow relevant health and safety standards, identify and correct worksite hazards, adequately inform employees about risks, provide protective equipment when necessary, keep accurate records of work-related injuries and illnesses, and report certain events to the government.

There is a trend toward exceeding these requirements and being proactive about general employee health by providing health-related services that are easily accessible to workers. The impact of occupational health efforts is not only a more productive, engaged workforce, but also a healthier population outside of the work setting.

THE ROLE OF NONCLINICAL PHYSICIANS

Occupational health requires an understanding of several subjects that are commonplace to clinical medicine, including pulmonology, dermatology, musculoskeletal disease, infectious disease, and mental health. Physicians who can approach these branches from a prevention and population-level management perspective are likely to succeed in an occupational health role.

185

Just as physicians in conventional patient care settings need to deliver care with consideration for payment systems and regulations, occupational health physicians must navigate administrative challenges, such as cost considerations and government compliance. Experience in any clinical setting is, therefore, relevant to occupational health work.

Many employers rely on physicians as the backbone of a strong employee health program. The industries most relevant to this field include those with notable hazards to employees, such as manufacturing, construction, transportation, mining and oil, agriculture and forestry, and utilities. However, professional, scientific, and other services industries use physicians for occupational health programs as well.

Employers
- Government agency, such as the Occupational Safety and Health Administration (OSHA)
- Large company in any industry
- Occupational health provider or consulting firm

JOB SUMMARY—DIRECTOR OF EMPLOYEE HEALTH AND SAFETY

Similar Job Titles
- Chief Medical Director
- Corporate Medical Director
- Director of Employee Health and Safety
- Director of Health Care Development
- Occupational Health Physician
- Plant Medical Director

The director of employee health and safety for a workplace provides administrative leadership for employee health and safety programs and services offered by the company. This job requires integrating preventive medicine and primary care principles with toxicology, industrial hygiene, safety techniques and practices, state and federal regulations, and company-specific operations.

Although much of a director's role concentrates on the overall employee population health, an individual health component often is required. If an onsite employee health clinic is available, the director ensures that its activities support the delivery of high-quality, cost-effective care and services.

The director works closely with company leadership, human resources professionals, industrial hygienists, and safety engineers on a range of workplace issues that affect employee health. The role involves interacting with government agencies regarding regulations and inspections. The director may collaborate with local health care providers and facilities to address medical needs related to employees.

A health and safety director may conduct surveillance or evaluations and recommend procedural changes or hazard controls in response to chemical exposures, poor ergonomic design, and other hazards. Even psychological hazards, such as a fatigue or workplace violence, may need to be addressed.

The precise responsibilities for the employee health and safety director at a corporation depend on the company's industry and the tasks the employees perform. In most cases, though, the director develops policies and procedures related to workplace injury and illness prevention and risk mitigation. A key challenge is using resources effectively and complying with regulations while simultaneously safeguarding employee health.

Example Responsibilities

- Ensure compliance with federal, state, and local regulations and with company policy
- Provide direction to human resources and management relating to company-level health issues
- Implement preventive measures for minimizing work-related disease, injuries, and exposures
- Perform reviews of incidents and analyze causal factors
- Contribute to worker health education efforts
- Perform mandated health- and safety-related surveillance and audits
- Identify and address unmet occupational health needs
- Consult with other physicians regarding employee health status

A NOTE ABOUT CLINICAL WORK

Many occupational health medical directors have some responsibility for direct employee care; however, companies with multiple locations, plants, or facilities often employ a corporate-level director to oversee their occupational health services company-wide.

Even a company with a single, large facility may hire health care providers, including nurse practitioners or physician assistants, to staff an employee clinic while a medical director focuses on administrative and oversight duties.

Still other companies rely on nearby health centers or hospitals for employees' acute medical needs. In these situations, a medical director may be responsible for OSHA-required exams, fitness-for-duty evaluations, and return-to-work readiness assessments, but not for treatment of acute injuries and occupational illnesses.

OTHER NONCLINICAL JOB OPTIONS

Occupational health consulting firms provide a spectrum of services, such as developing health-related procedures and policies, leading training courses, conducting worksite inspections and audits, and investigating incidents. They may be called on to put programs and measures in place proactively or to investigate and respond to actual instances of exposures or injuries. Physician consultants perform similar work to a director of employee health and safety, but have the opportunity to do so for several clients.

CAREERS WITH AN ENVIRONMENTAL HEALTH FOCUS

An environmental health officer in a public health setting responds to chemical and biologic environmental exposures, implements measures to prevent environmental health risks, and communicates with the public about these risks. This individual may be involved in tracking air quality, disease-carrying vectors, and food and water safety.

Scientific consulting firms offer another option for physicians in environmental health. These firms assist companies with challenges related to their environmental practices or hazardous materials use by performing risk assessments and providing data-backed solutions. They usually offer interdisciplinary expertise from scientists, engineers, lawyers, regulatory specialists, and medical professionals.

QUALIFICATIONS

An active medical license and board certification may be required if responsibilities include advising on worker treatment of exposures or work-related diseases.

Occupational medicine (colloquially known as *occ med*) is an American Board of Medical Specialties–recognized specialty. Although board certification can make a candidate competitive for positions in occupational health, it often is not a necessity—especially for nonclinical roles.

Some jobs in this field require an MPH or other public health training.

COMPENSATION

Salary in this field varies by job responsibilities. The size of the employee population and occupational health division also affect compensation.

Jobs with a clinical oversight component requiring an active medical license are likely to pay higher, with salaries rivaling or exceeding that of primary care work.

Director of Employee Health and Safety

37. Epidemiology and Disease Surveillance

Epidemiology is the study of the distribution and determinants of health and disease conditions in defined populations. It is a core science of public health. It can be used to analyze the health or disease burden in a community, to score individual health risks, to identify syndrome clusters, and to search for causes of morbidity.

Disease surveillance is one of the most commonly used practices in epidemiology. By monitoring disease spread and progression patterns, it assists in predicting, observing, and minimizing the harm caused by disease, including outbreaks and epidemics.

Health surveillance historically has focused on infectious disease but has expanded to include a wide range of health outcomes and their determinants. These include chronic diseases, injuries, and health behaviors. Although the leading causes of death in the United States have shifted to noncommunicable causes, infectious disease epidemiology remains relevant. Population growth, global travel, risky human behaviors, and changing environmental conditions favor infectious disease spread.

Epidemiologic practice and the results of epidemiologic analysis make a widespread impact. They support structure and processes within health care systems, influencing patient care training, planning, and programming. They contribute to emerging population-based health management frameworks. In government settings, they affect political decisions, budget and resource allocations, personnel selection, and legislation.

THE ROLE OF NONCLINICAL PHYSICIANS

Medical training is an excellent context for epidemiology and disease surveillance. Knowledge of disease causation, diagnosis, treatment, and prognosis is important for both analyzing surveillance data and applying its results.

A clinical background is advantageous in understanding health care practices as they apply to diseases and in working with clinical stakeholders to develop surveillance efforts.

Employers
- Government agency
- Government contractor
- Local or state department of health
- University

JOB SUMMARY—MEDICAL EPIDEMIOLOGIST

Similar Job Titles
- Clinical Epidemiologist
- Director of Health Surveillance
- Epidemiologist
- Scientific Director of Epidemiology
- Surveillance Advisor

Given their extensive training and health care experience, physicians working as epidemiologists often oversee entire programs. In doing so, they may supervise a team of MPH- and nurse-level epidemiologists as well as statisticians and administrative support staff. A program typically focuses on a certain disease area or health topic that requires ongoing surveillance.

Developing and utilizing a surveillance system requires clear objectives and case definitions, data collection mechanisms, testing, an analytical approach, and a data interpretation strategy. To effectively apply the results of disease surveillance efforts, collaboration with teams within and outside the organization is needed. Consequently, physician epidemiologists take on a number of roles, including planner, evaluator, communicator, and coordinator.

Example Responsibilities
- Oversee data collection and analysis as part of a surveillance program
- Serve as a liaison to health systems regarding disease surveillance programs and response
- Lead projects focused on improving disease surveillance

- Conduct epidemiologic studies using a variety of data sources
- Serve as a subject matter expert for targeted health conditions
- Manage databases to track diseases, programs, risk factors, and outcomes
- Conduct literature reviews and prepare reports related to surveillance data
- Assess target populations, health disparities, and disease spread characteristics
- Communicate results of surveillance and evaluation activities
- Provide medical input into programs, analyses, and applications

OTHER NONCLINICAL JOB OPTIONS

There are several branches of epidemiology, each with distinct workforce needs. Pharmacoepidemiology is one area that requires MD-level expertise and tends to appeal to physicians seeking nonclinical work. Positions in this field often are drug safety roles with pharmaceutical companies, but such positions also exist in academia and the public sector.

QUALIFICATIONS

Epidemiologist qualifications are quite varied. Many positions require a doctoral degree. The need for medical specialty training varies by organization and program type.

An MPH or other public health degree sometimes is mandatory. If not required, experience in applying epidemiologic and biostatistics principles strengthens a candidate's application.

COMPENSATION

Variations in compensation are mainly due to differences in degree and training requirements. Roles requiring a medical degree naturally are paid more.

Many opportunities for physicians in this field are in governmental positions and, therefore, are subject to established pay scales.

Medical Epidemiologist

38. Health Policy and Politics

Public policy outlines priorities and expected roles for governmental and, to a lesser extent, nongovernmental groups. It informs people and builds consensus in achieving a vision for the future. Policy formation and adoption ultimately helps the United States, its citizens, its businesses, and other nations find solutions to common problems and ways to pay for them.

Health policy, more specifically, is composed of the decisions, plans, and actions taken to achieve societal health-related goals. It encompasses public health policy, health services policy, and global health policy, among other types.

Politics is "the authoritative allocation of values" for society.[28] It is guided by political science, which attempts to reveal the laws that govern political behavior and provide objective, empirical evidence for the rules that help policymakers solve problems.

Through political activities, the government puts measures in place that encourage people and organizations to contribute to society and to cooperate when necessary, while simultaneously protecting rights and liberties. It employs the tools of command, veto power, agenda control, voting rules, and delegation to do so.

THE ROLE OF NONCLINICAL PHYSICIANS

With rapid technological growth and scientific advances, there is a need for scientific policy expertise—much of it related to health and medicine. Physicians in this field can draw on their subject matter expertise in the context of the economic and social consequences of policy decisions.

Evidence-based policy is a term in the field of political science that is comparable to the term *evidence-based medicine*. It refers to situations whereby policy decisions are informed by rigorously established objective information. The practice of being guided by objectivity is routine for physicians, arming them to use a similar approach in health policy careers and political appointments.

Several federal government agencies as well as state and local offices offer opportunities in health policy, although job options for physicians in this field are not restricted to the government. Research institutions, universities, consulting organizations, and think tanks study complex problems and recommend solutions in hopes of influencing government action. For many organizations, demand is growing for staff who are highly educated and experienced scientific and technical specialists.

Physicians in politics must consider their skills broadly, because elected public positions are wide-ranging, and only a portion of the work focuses on health topics. Having spent so many years learning and honing skills in medicine shouldn't turn physicians off from political positions, because the system and rules can be learned by those who are not career-long politicians. Voters value "real" people who understand their problems and have lived through situations similar to their own.

Employers
- Academic institution
- Consulting firm
- Governmental affairs or political affairs department of a large company
- Governmental agency or department
- Health-related foundation
- Policy research institute or think tank

JOB SUMMARY—HEALTH POLICY ANALYST

Similar Job Titles
- Health Policy Advisor
- Health Policy Director
- Policy Research Director

A health policy analyst is responsible for analyzing and developing policy, regulations, or legislation. This can be at the national or state level. The issues addressed are determined by the organization type and its needs, mission, and funding sources.

An analyst assesses the impact of proposed policy changes on physicians, patients, the general public, medical practice, and health care delivery. Analyzing the effects of a new health technology, for example, may prompt changes to existing regulations that would affect the technology's availability or use.

A health policy analyst's work is shared with a broad audience that includes policymakers, the media, and the public. Analysts often testify, provide oral briefings to government officials, and speak publicly. They disseminate their findings through publications such as white papers and editorials. They may be asked for an expert opinion on someone else's proposed policy changes and to respond to public inquiries.

At think tanks and other nongovernmental organizations, an analyst may be tasked with recommending new initiatives and identifying funding opportunities.

Example Responsibilities

- Monitor for emerging trends, legislative items, statutes, and regulatory action
- Analyze legislative initiatives for their impact on medicine and health care
- Develop documents that outline key issues and propose courses of action and alternatives
- Conduct research on policy priorities
- Confer with officials and relevant organizations about policy topics
- Communicate with Congressional staff about issues of interest
- Serve as an internal and external point person for policy issues
- Review policy position white papers, lobbying materials, and other documents

OTHER NONCLINICAL JOB OPTIONS

Elected public official positions of interest to physicians range from local to federal and differ greatly with regard to scope and commitment. The choice of which office to run for will be guided by the issues the candidate is passionate about, as well as logistics and long-term career goals.

Elected positions that occasionally are held by physicians include U.S. Congress member, state governor, city mayor, and county commissioner.

The U.S. House of Representatives consists of members who are elected by popular vote to serve two-year terms representing a district. Although there are not many physicians in Congress, they proportionately over-represent physicians in the United States.[29]

A House member has duties in several functional areas, including local representation, constituency service, legislation, investigation, and over-sight management. A principal function of representatives is making law, which involves originating bills, studying bills' effects, proposing amendments, persuading others to support a point of view, and voting. Representatives must do this all while keeping the best interest of their home district citizens in mind.

An interesting aspect of public office jobs is that, to a large degree, the elected public official is free to define his or her own priorities.

QUALIFICATIONS

A medical degree is not required for careers in health policy or politics, although it can help in both landing a job and being successful at it.

Most policy analysts have a doctoral or other graduate degree. More important than the degree itself is being knowledgeable about the policy environment and the issues affecting it.

The basic requirements for elected public positions are straightforward. A congress member, for example, needs only to be at least 25 years old, a U.S. citizen for seven years, and a resident of the state they're represent-ing. Convincing the public of one's suitability for the position is more complicated. Physicians may have somewhat of a leg up when running for office by having a respected degree and by being known in the com-munity through a medical practice.

COMPENSATION

Doctoral-level jobs in health policy are well-paid, although compensa-tion is unlikely to match clinical work salaries.

Compensation for governmental health policy jobs and elected public offices varies by position but is firm for each position due to government pay scales. These jobs, though, are accompanied by strong benefits packages.

Physicians running for office need to be prepared for campaigning efforts and expenses.

Health Policy Analyst

U.S. Congress Representative

39. Criminal Justice and Forensic Science

The U.S. criminal justice system is comprised of law enforcement, the courts, and corrections. Forensic science is the study and application of science to matters related to law. It includes the disciplines of forensic pathology, forensic toxicology, and forensic psychology. The term *forensic medicine* has been used to encompass the field of medicine as it relates to these branches.

Criminal justice and forensic science have increased in importance in parallel with growing attention to civil liberties and human rights matters. Moreover, the incarceration rate in the United States rose dramatically in the 1980s through the 2000s. Although it has decreased since then, it remains the highest in the world.[30]

Health care plays a role in several overarching aspects of the criminal justice system, as well as in the lives of almost all individuals who are involved in the system. This is primarily in corrections, in which a jurisdiction is responsible for the health care needs of their incarcerated population.

Correctional health care is challenged by an aging population and high rates of mental illness, trauma, infectious disease, and substance abuse. Trends in the field include health care service privatization, efforts aimed at reducing recidivism, and use of telemedicine to improve care and address security concerns.

THE ROLE OF NONCLINICAL PHYSICIANS

Incarcerated individuals retain the basic rights of access to health care, professional medical judgment, and receipt of care ordered by a health care provider. However, having lost certain rights and privileges, they are a vulnerable population. Medical care in the correctional setting encompasses treatment of the same acute and chronic conditions with which all of us are experienced, but also must deal with nuances such as managing physical injuries incurred during or after arrest.

Qualified medical professionals are needed in this field, not only to deliver care but to develop, implement, and improve systems and processes that adequately address this population's health needs.

Outside of the corrections setting, physician expertise comes into play wherever a crime involves a health-related outcome or death. Pathologists and psychiatrists have the most opportunity within forensic science, although doctors in other specialties can find a niche, too. For example, physicians with a biology-heavy background can contribute to the field of forensic toxicology, which involves investigating the effects of toxins and drugs on the body.

Employers
- Federal Bureau of Prisons
- Private correctional health care provider
- State Department of Corrections
- State or county government department

JOB SUMMARY—MEDICAL PROGRAM ADMINISTRATOR

Similar Job Titles
- Chief Medical Officer
- Corporate Medical Director
- Regional or Statewide Medical Director

A medical program administrator has overall accountability for quality and cost of medical care provided to the offender population in a department of corrections or a jurisdiction. By virtue of having a defined patient population in a restricted setting, a jail or prison meets inmate health needs through a structure that roughly corresponds to that of the health care system in the community. For the medical program administrator, this creates responsibilities that are similar to aspects of nonclinical physician positions in managed care, utilization management, public health, and health care organization leadership.

This job involves establishing health care policies and programming that meet a necessary scope and standard of services, which can depend on federal, state, and local laws as well as accrediting body standards.

It is challenging to deliver quality health care services in a correctional setting while maintaining alignment with custody-related policies and safety requirements. A medical program administrator is the voice of the department's clinical staff in advocating for health care service needs. This requires identifying and addressing barriers to effectively and efficiently delivering care.

Corrections can be a tough working environment with a high staff turnover. A medical administrator must nurture a culture of engaged health care staff and may be involved in the hiring and training a team of medical professionals.

Program administrators foster external relationships. Contracts with local hospitals and medical specialists are needed for times when patient medical needs exceed a facility's capabilities. Community public health departments have an interest in patient linkage to care following release. The court and law enforcement system may seek guidance and training on matters relating to offender health needs.

Example Responsibilities
- Oversee and develop health care programs consistent with agency priorities
- Develop and execute a talent management strategy to attract and retain health care staff
- Ensure that health services meet necessary standards
- Provide consultation in the event of a critical incident affecting inmate health
- Liaise and contract with outside hospitals and specialist physicians
- Participate in quality improvement initiatives and mortality reviews
- Develop drug formularies and interpret trends in medication use and costs
- Address patient and family member grievances
- Monitor utilization of specialty and acute care delivered outside of the facility

OTHER NONCLINICAL JOB OPTIONS

Medical examiner is one of the most common positions for physicians relating to forensic science. A medical examiner investigates deaths and injuries that occur under suspicious or unnatural circumstances and performs post-mortems. This involves evaluating the medical history and physical findings of the deceased and factors surrounding the death. It requires examining crime scenes, performing autopsies or evaluating autopsy reports, and reviewing laboratory and radiologic data. Consulting with medical and professional personnel in other fields, such as toxicology, may be required. In some cases, medical examiners are asked to testify in court. Similar job titles include chief physician, chief medical examiner, and physician specialist.

QUALIFICATIONS

A medical license typically is required for any physician leadership position in correctional health care, due to clinician oversight and the inevitable involvement in patient care decisions from time to time.

Training or experience in public health, certification as a Certified Correctional Health Professional, and prior clinical experience in a correctional setting may be preferred or required.

In many jurisdictions, a medical examiner is required not only to hold an MD, but also to have pathology training.

COMPENSATION

Salaries are on par with primary care. Physicians employed by government entities in this field may earn less than physicians in similar positions with for-profit companies.

Medical Program Administrator

Medical Examiner

PHYSICIAN PROFILE:

Mike Davis, MD, PhD

JOB TITLE: Lead Physician (Clinical Team Leader)

EMPLOYER: U.S. Food and Drug Administration

What does your organization do?

The Division of Psychiatry Products is in the Office of New Drugs, which is part of the FDA Center for Drug Evaluation and Research. We provide regulatory oversight for investigational studies during drug development, decide whether to approve new drugs for marketing, regulate drug labeling to ensure it contains essential scientific information needed for the safe and effective use of drugs, and provide guidance to the pharmaceutical industry on clinical, scientific, and regulatory matters related to drug development.

The scope of our activities is within the therapeutic area of psychiatry and, as such, we regulate drugs developed for the treatment of psychiatric disorders, including schizophrenia, major depressive disorder, anxiety disorders, and attention deficit hyperactivity disorder.

What is your role within the organization?

I lead a small team of four to five psychiatrists who serve as the primary clinical reviewers on regulatory work in the division, including new drug applications (NDAs), investigational new drug applications (INDs), and other regulatory documents.

What are your responsibilities?

As a clinical team leader, I serve as a principal advisor to the division director and other FDA managers. Specifically, I assign and review the work of primary clinical reviewers on my team, perform a secondary clinical review on certain projects, such as NDAs, and provide instruction and guidance to team members on review work. I am involved in special projects, such as writing guidance documents and providing subject matter expertise in collaborative projects involving other FDA centers or offices.

Prior to becoming a team leader, my responsibilities as a primary clinical reviewer included reviewing new IND applications and NDAs, responding to questions in formal meetings between the FDA and pharmaceutical companies, reviewing clinical trial protocols, reviewing applications to change labeling of currently approved drugs, and providing subject matter consultation to other groups within the FDA.

When we review NDAs (perhaps the highest profile work we do), we assess the body of clinical trial data submitted with an application as to whether there is a favorable balance between benefits and risks with the drug to support marketing approval.

What does a typical day on the job look like?

I'm involved in several activities during a typical day. I evaluate clinical review documents drafted by team members and provide feedback on their content and format prior to signing off on their completion.

I may have meetings of various types. In one-to-one meetings with team members, we discuss their ongoing work assignments. I attend multidisciplinary internal meetings to discuss reviews of INDs, NDAs, and other team-based work assignments. I participate in meetings between our division and pharmaceutical companies to discuss their planned or ongoing drug development programs.

Work on special projects takes up a portion of my day. This might include internal research projects, writing new FDA guidance documents, or making slides for external conference presentations.

How does your medical background and experience contribute to your work?

My medical background and experience provide the foundation for clinical review work. Specific activities that rely on medical training include assessing whether proposed clinical trial protocols with investigational drugs are reasonably safe to proceed, interpreting safety data from clinical trials to characterize safety signals that inform regulatory decisions, and assessing the clinical meaningfulness of improvements on rating scales used to demonstrate the therapeutic benefit of a new drug.

Although they were not required for my clinical reviewer position, both my prior graduate training in pharmacology and my fellowship training in schizophrenia clinical research have a positive impact on the work I do by providing additional knowledge and experience with data analysis, clinical trial methodology, and scientific writing.

What are the best parts of your job?

I enjoy learning about novel treatments and mechanisms of action and having an important role in the overall drug development process. I enjoy working in teams of intelligent professionals across many disciplines, including statistics, toxicology, clinical pharmacology, and chemistry, because I am constantly learning new things.

It is fulfilling to contribute to the field of clinical psychiatry by making regulatory decisions that affect the development, availability, and labeling of new treatments to ensure they are safe and effective for patients.

What are the main challenges you face?

Much of the work we do in our division has statutory deadlines for completion. For example, there is a 30-day safety review window for new INDs and user fee–associated deadlines for reviewing NDAs. Depending on the volume and timing of regulatory submissions and the level of staffing in our division, it can be stressful working on many complex projects in parallel to ensure they are completed by their mandated deadlines while meeting quality standards.

Where might your career go from here?

It is difficult to say at this point, but I currently have no plans to leave the FDA. A nice feature of working at the FDA is the opportunity (with supervisor agreement) to be detailed to work in other agency positions for limited periods. These detail positions can be useful for gaining knowledge and experience that can be brought back to the regular position or for exploring positions to pursue as part of a career development path within the agency.

What are some considerations for physicians interested in a nonclinical career with the FDA or in other areas of the federal government?

The FDA is a large organization. Between 8000 and 9000 employees work at the main FDA campus. Physicians can fill many different position types.

I have found that a number of characteristics and qualities are associated with thriving in a clinical reviewer position within a therapeutic area drug review division. These include interest in and curiosity about topics related to drug development, scientific and analytic thinking skills, and the ability to collaborate effectively in multidisciplinary teams. Good organization and time management skills are important, because clinical reviewers often work on multiple projects simultaneously, with deadlines ranging from days to weeks to months. It also is helpful to enjoy (or at least tolerate) computer-based data analysis (with training and support), reading, thinking, and writing.

Currently, physicians need to have a medical degree and completion of a residency training program within the specialty of the position, or equivalent experience and training.

Characteristics of physician jobs vary across HHS agencies and across specific positions within agencies, in terms of both the day-to-day work content and organizational culture. Thus, I recommend communicating with relevant staff from the agency of interest to learn more about different job opportunities for physicians.

The government hiring process and timeline differs significantly from nongovernment positions. If you are interested in a career at the FDA or another government agency, I recommend you start the job search and application process much earlier than you would for traditional clinical positions, to allow plenty of time for completion of the government hiring process. In addition, there generally is less flexibility in negotiating terms of a government job, such as salary and relocation benefits, than there may be for jobs in the private sector.

Education and Research

areers for physicians in education and research exist both in and out of academia. *Academia* is a collective term encompassing the work of those engaged in scholarly activities, such as education and research at colleges, universities, and medical schools. A career in education or research—or one that combines the two—is an opportunity to contribute to scientific knowledge and guide the next generation of physicians, scientists, and health care professionals.

Universities follow a hierarchical ranking structure for professors and certain other academic staff that is standard across the institution. Within that hierarchy, many faculty have (or are pursuing) tenure. Tenure-track professors typically begin as assistant professors and progress to associate professor before attaining full professor rank. To progress, they are required to demonstrate that they've made contributions to their discipline and to the school.

Academic faculty tend to split their time among teaching, research, and service to the institution. The relative importance of each depends on the position, departmental needs, and funding sources. For physicians, patient care often is added to the mix; however, there are plenty of opportunities without clinical obligations for both tenured faculty and nontenured staff.

It is common to hear someone described as "an academic" as though there is no hope of ever leaving academia. In reality, though, physicians with experience in research and higher education are well-equipped to transition between academia and industry or government roles.

40. Teaching

The U.S. higher education system is diverse. There are public and private institutions, ranging from small to large, in urban, suburban, and rural locations. Some are secular, and some have a religious affiliation. Each has an individual mission to disseminate knowledge.

As our understanding of the human body and how it interacts with the world deepens, the need for knowledgeable individuals to teach the next cohorts of scientists and health care professionals continues to expand.

THE ROLE OF NONCLINICAL PHYSICIANS

A doctorate degree of any type is a suitable background for many higher education teaching positions. Extensive training in biology and medical science makes physicians particularly suited for teaching at medical schools, schools of public health, and health sciences schools. Programs in nursing, physician assisting, and pharmacy also rely on physicians to teach complex subjects related to medicine.

Employers
- College
- Public or private university

JOB SUMMARY—TEACHING FACULTY

Similar Job Titles
- Adjunct Faculty
- Assistant, Associate, or full Professor
- Instructor
- Lecturer

University teaching faculty are responsible for fostering the knowledge and skills necessary for students' success in both their degree programs and professional practice. This primarily involves planning and delivering course content to students through lectures, small group sessions, labs, and online formats.

Teaching faculty develop and review assignments and assessments to evaluate student knowledge. They provide feedback and support through holding office hours or answering questions asynchronously via online learning platforms. They work with teaching assistants and instructors to coordinate learning activities for courses.

In addition to teaching courses, teaching faculty dedicate a portion of their time to departmental-level duties and mentoring individual students. They may participate in recruiting activities, advise students, supervise student projects, and establish community partnerships for experiential learning opportunities.

Tenure-track faculty have more responsibility for service to the institution than instructors who are not vying for tenure. They may also be expected to participate in research or other scholarly activities.

Example Responsibilities

- Teach courses in one or more subject areas
- Work collaboratively with faculty to ensure consistency and alignment between courses
- Evaluate, grade, and give feedback to students
- Seek and secure opportunities for grants, collaborative projects, and interprofessional activities

QUALIFICATIONS

Medical school faculty generally are required to hold a doctorate. Depending on the discipline, a medical degree may be required or preferred over a PhD. Faculty in other types of higher education, such as ancillary health programs, may instead hold the degree awarded by the program, a master's degree, or other credential.

Academic appointments without clinical responsibilities rarely require an active medical license.

Faculty candidates are expected to have demonstrated interest in teaching and often are asked to share a pedagogical statement or teaching philosophy.

COMPENSATION

Teaching faculty rank and salary depend on qualifications and experience. Universities have established parameters on the necessary criteria for appointment to each academic rank within their faculty system.

Salary for academic teaching positions does not compete with that of clinical faculty. Nonetheless, several nonmonetary advantages can make a teaching career attractive. "University professor" was rated as one of the ten least stressful jobs by a 2018 CareerCast study.[31] Teaching faculty have considerable flexibility in their day-to-day schedules and often receive generous time off in alignment with the school's academic calendar.

Teaching Faculty

Instructor

Medical School and Professional School Administration

Whereas faculty are hired to teach for a university, administrators are hired to think for the university.

Higher education has changed in structure and scope over the years. Focus on financial health and prestige has amplified for colleges and universities of all types. Academic institutions have become complex and open to public scrutiny. As a result, demands on higher education leadership are increased in the setting of limited resources.

Medical schools and health professional schools depend on skilled administrators to oversee their offices of academic, student, faculty, community, career, and alumni affairs. Deans, directors, and other leaders support the school's mission and the functions that are integral to running a medical or health degree-granting program.

University administrators have a unique opportunity to facilitate the many moving parts of a university in aligning and working together. As opposed to faculty who pursue their own research, teaching, or clinical agenda, administrators work for the success of the school.

THE ROLE OF NONCLINICAL PHYSICIANS

The Liaison Committee on Medical Education (LCME), which accredits medical schools, requires that deans be qualified by their education and experience to provide leadership in medical education. Thus, most medical school dean positions are filled by physicians.

Even where a medical degree is not required for accreditation purposes, medical education and clinical experience is important. Special programs or new initiatives at a medical school often do not fit squarely into an existing individual's job description. They may require a new director for initiative development and oversight. Physicians have a relevant background for such roles and a degree of immediate respect among faculty members.

Medical and health professional schools have excellent career opportunities for physicians who can excel at the intersection of management, academics, and medicine. Although some physicians in administrator positions continue to teach, practice clinically, or do research, many simply don't have time for this or are not required to continue these activities.

Employers

- Medical school
- School of nursing or health sciences

JOB SUMMARY—ASSOCIATE DEAN FOR STUDENT AFFAIRS

The senior administrator over a school of higher education is the dean. Associate deans are given responsibility over an institutional office or functional area, and are roughly equivalent in seniority to vice presidents in industry. The associate dean for student affairs has primary responsibility for the programs, policies, management, and services that support students.

Similar Job Titles

- Assistant Dean for Student Affairs
- Associate Dean for Student Development
- Associate Dean for Student Services
- Vice President of Student Affairs

Associate deans are subject to the powers of the board and priorities of the dean, yet closely involved with the daily goings-on of the school. In a sense, the associate dean for student affairs is a liaison between the students and the institution.

Because most school activities involve or affect students, a diverse array of issues lands on an associate dean's desk. These range in importance and complexity, often requiring the associate dean to work closely with administrative leaders in academic departments and various offices, such as admissions or alumni relations.

Duties include career advising, assisting new students in becoming acclimated, ensuring general student well-being, and overseeing school-wide events, such as commencement. From an outward-facing perspective, the associate dean may be involved in strengthening partnerships with affiliated institutions, community practices, and professional associations.

Example Responsibilities

- Oversee all operations of the student affairs office
- Serve as a representative on relevant committees
- Ensure that students are provided support, counseling, and discipline as needed
- Develop administrative policies and procedures that contribute to student success
- Prepare student performance evaluations and monitor probationary statuses
- Serve as a representative to the Association of American Medical Colleges (AAMC) and other organizations
- Manage an operational budget for student affairs activities
- Oversee orientation, the residency match process, commencement, and other activities

As associate deans, physicians are unlikely to work alongside students on a daily basis in the same way they do in teaching positions. Rather, their impact lies in broadly supporting students, faculty, and staff and in designing and maintaining programs that help fulfill their goals and meet their needs.

An individual in this role must share the institution's vision. An associate dean works with agendas that may not be his or her own. There may be upset faculty and students that need their concerns heard. There may be budget cuts, layoffs, and enrollment issues that affect the office's priorities and capabilities.

JOB SUMMARY—DIRECTOR OF LEARNING AND INNOVATION

Similar Job Titles

- Director of Assessment
- Director of Leadership Development
- Director of Simulation and Standardized Patient Education

A cross between a teacher and administrator, the director of a center for learning and innovation has responsibility for shaping the approaches used in medical education. Methods and styles used in medical education need to be kept up to date with educational research, advances in learning technologies, and trends in pedagogies.

A center focused on innovation in learning may be involved with online and distance learning programs, simulation labs, standardized patient programs, and use of immersive technologies for medical education. The director defines the center's strategy, leads its mission, and works to integrate its learning experiences with the school's basic and clinical science curriculums.

Example Responsibilities

- Direct the overall programming and services offered by a learning center
- Guide vision and strategy for use of learning technologies within the school
- Ensure best practices in educational experience development and delivery
- Provide medical and clinical expertise in the design of curricula and assessments
- Work with students and residents in learning and remediating skills
- Oversee the center's budget and seek funding and grant support
- Evaluate program activity outcomes and impact on student performance

OTHER NONCLINICAL JOB OPTIONS

At a small school, an associate dean might be one of few administrators at their level and wear many hats. Larger schools can have a dozen or more associate deans and directors. These include:

- **Associate dean for academic affairs.** Responsible for maintaining acceptable academic standards, including both didactic instruction and clinical practice experience.
- **Associate dean for admissions.** Contributes to all aspects of the admissions process, including recruitment efforts, application and interview procedures, and student selection.
- **Associate dean for faculty.** Oversees initiatives to support the school's faculty, including professional development, advancing standards of collegiality and collaboration between faculty members, and acting as the voice of faculty within administration.

QUALIFICATIONS

Senior administrators in schools of higher education have track records of involvement and recognition in academia. Most associate dean positions require eligibility for a particular academic appointment or rank. The traditional administrator path starts with serving as a department chair. Many associate deans have deviated from a path toward becoming a full professor in order to focus on administration.

The search for medical and health science professional school leadership can be long, arduous, and quite political.

It is more important that medical school leadership be competent in the administrative aspects of medical education than that they be clinically competent. Slowly working up to a senior-level position or having decades of clinical experience is not always necessary to land and succeed in a medical school administration position.

The qualifications for a director position, such as the director of learning and innovation, may be less stringent than that for an associate dean. Tenure eligibility or even a medical degree may not be required, although this depends on the institution and specifics of the position.

COMPENSATION

Given LCME's requirement for leaders who are qualified in medical education, medical school associate dean salaries can rival those for clinical work. Compensation for other administrative roles or associate dean positions at other types of professional schools may be lower.

It is common for top-level administrators in higher education to transition between schools, which can be accompanied by enticing compensation and relocation packages.

Associate Dean for Student Affairs

Director of Learning and Innovation

42. Biomedical Research

Biomedical research commonly is divided into basic and clinical research. Basic (or "bench") research aims to increase understanding of fundamental principles and mechanisms that govern human biology. It is directed toward greater knowledge and understanding of science and phenomena, without considering practical ends. Its potential bearing on patient care and health may not be immediately clear.

Clinical (or "bedside") research is applied research that directly involves people or tissue samples, often with an intervention that may affect human behavior or the body's physiologic or pathologic processes. Clinical research often is conducted by physicians alongside clinical work or by biopharmaceutical companies.

Translational research, which builds on basic research to apply its findings and translate them into medical practice, also lies within the realm of biomedical research.

This is an overly simplistic classification, however. Molecular biology, medical genetics, immunology, neurosciences, psychology, and other research fields each have distinctive methodologies and nuances.

THE ROLE OF NONCLINICAL PHYSICIANS

Physician-scientists are a crucial component of biomedical research. Most of us have been involved in basic or beside research at some point in our careers or training. A thorough understanding of biologic processes, diseases, and patient needs equips physicians to ask applicable research questions, design suitable experiments, and analyze results.

Most jobs for physicians in biomedical research are in academia, although some exist in independent research institutes, such as those funded by charitable trusts and corporations. The NIH invests over $30 billion annually in medical research through competitive grants awarded to medical schools, universities, and research institutions.[32] As a result, it is not difficult for physicians to find opportunities in this field.

Employers
- Independent research institute
- Medical school
- University

JOB SUMMARY—RESEARCH PROFESSOR

Similar Job Titles
- Assistant, Associate, or full Professor

Academic researchers whose work is supported by external grants often are tenure-track faculty, a category that includes the titles Assistant Professor, Associate Professor, and full Research Professor.

A professor's research activities include identifying and applying for grant funding, coordinating lab or research center projects, and communicating findings. In an academic setting, research is guided by funding availability within a topic area and by the researcher's intellectual curiosity.

Compared with industry research roles, there is more flexibility in the type of research conducted and less urgency to get it done. Nonetheless, a research professor has to show progress. Professors also are expected to demonstrate professional growth to be promoted up the ranks of professorship. This can require service to the university, involvement in the professional community, and scholarly activities. Research professors also may be expected to teach courses or give seminars related to their research fields.

Example Responsibilities
- Identify research funding opportunities and apply for grants
- Design and implement research protocols
- Conduct experiments to answer posed research questions
- Confer with biostatisticians about data analyses
- Write and edit manuscripts for publication in journals
- Present research findings internally and externally

- Manage the staff, equipment, and budget for a research lab
- Collaborate with investigators on joint research projects

OTHER NONCLINICAL JOB OPTIONS

Non-tenured Research Jobs

Some research positions in academia do not require faculty appointment, such as research associate, research scientist, and research instructor. These researchers work under the direction of a faculty member who serves as the principal investigator for the research being conducted. Positions usually are funded by a grant awarded to the principal investigator.

Whereas faculty may be pulled in different directions across their departments and institutions, research associates and similar employed staff can focus on performing research and generating results. Positions requiring a doctoral-level degree can have a high responsibility level. Research associates make substantial scholarly contributions by means of identifying research questions, planning experiments, and interpreting and publishing results. They may have overall responsibility for managing a lab, including supervising technical staff, budgeting, and maintaining lab safety.

Medical school clinical departments sometimes hire doctoral-level researchers to advance their research missions. These jobs often focus on translational research and aim to move research toward actual disease treatment within the lab's affiliated hospitals and clinics.

Research Administration Jobs

Physicians may find their backgrounds and interests are fitting for work in research administrative roles. Technology commercialization, for example, acts as the bridge between academic research centers and corporations or startup companies. Experience in this area can open up doors to jobs in venture capital and legal consulting.

QUALIFICATIONS

A degree and an interest in biomedical research are sufficient to land many research jobs. However, for some positions, additional training or experience may be required or preferred.

A combined MD/PhD is beneficial for many positions. A PhD demonstrates proficiency in research techniques as well as critical thinking skills that differ from those used in medical practice.

COMPENSATION

Biomedical research does not pay as well as clinical work, but is generally less stressful, while still being stimulating and mentally rewarding.

Research professor salaries vary by rank, institution type, and research discipline. Non-tenured faculty researchers tend to earn less than professors.

Research Professor

Research Associate

Health Services Research

The goals of health care's "triple aim"—to increase access, improve quality, and reduce costs—often compete with one another. Achieving them while maintaining balance remains a challenge for health care institutions.

A health system consists of not just the service of delivering care, but a workforce, a health information system, medical products and technologies, financing, and governance. There are many moving parts. Although there is a general consensus that strengthening health systems is necessary to improve the population's health, the best way to accomplish this is unclear. This has led to development of the relatively young field of health services research.

Health services research has been defined as "the study of how social factors, financing systems, organizational structures and processes, health technologies, and personal behaviors affect access to health care, the quality and cost of health care, and ultimately our health." [33] It influences how health care is delivered in an effort to improve outcomes and ensure that we are providing high-value services.

THE ROLE OF NONCLINICAL PHYSICIANS

Physicians who cannot stomach basic research and who are not interested in directly treating patients do not need to dismiss research as a fulfilling career option. Physicians have experienced the health care system in multiple settings, as professionals, trainees, and patients. The field of health services research benefits from the multidisciplinary experience and knowledge of researchers who are passionate about improving health care on a broad scale.

A health services research center may have very few researchers with clinical experience. Physicians in this setting can provide clinical insight in study design and execution.

The need for health services research has many drivers, and numerous stakeholders are involved. As a result, there are several types of organizations in which health services research is conducted, and various funding sources that support such research.

Academia is a major source of jobs for physicians in this field. Although federal funding is limited, a number of government agencies recognize the need for health services research and expend funds for studies and related activities. These include HHS, the Veterans Health Administration, and the Department of Defense.[34] Private sector careers in health services research may involve federal contract work or be self-funded.

Employers
- Academic medical center
- Consulting firm
- Government office or agency
- Health insurance company
- Independent research institute
- Pharmaceutical company
- Professional society
- School of medicine, public health, or health professions
- Think tank

JOB SUMMARY—HEALTH SERVICES RESEARCH CENTER DIRECTOR

Similar Job Titles
- Assistant, Associate, or full Professor
- Executive Director
- Health Services Researcher
- Research Manager

Serving as a convener and facilitator to lead and grow the center's research activities, a health services research center director works to promote a collaborative and interdisciplinary program focused on evaluating the health services topics and questions of interest to the organization. These might include health care financing, health disparities, or the organization of health care. The topics of focus are driven by the center's mission and may be guided by external funding sources.

For new or evolving research programs, the director is charged with developing and implementing an overall plan for structure and staffing. This requires overseeing staff with backgrounds in public health, public policy, behavioral and social science, economics, and data science.

The center director ensures that research questions posed are informed by current practices, published research and literature, and relevant conceptual and theoretical models. Offering input on data analysis and dissemination ensures the center's goals are met. A physician in this role also provides clinical and health care expertise.

Leading or supporting internal and external collaborations is important for many health services research institutes, and an area in which the director is vital. Partnerships can be with industry, academic institutions, government, or professional organizations. These relationships guide the translation of research findings into policy and practice.

Example Responsibilities
- Ensure that research meets mission-driven goals
- Engage experts and stakeholders to inform research plans and priorities
- Work with research staff to execute studies and analyze results
- Identify means to incentivize new health services research activities and funding
- Produce manuscripts and presentations to disseminate research findings
- Promote the center as a resource for quality health services research and insight
- Ensure research is in compliance with funding requirements and ethical standards

OTHER NONCLINICAL JOB OPTIONS

Physicians without interest in a leadership position may be suited for a job as a health services research associate or research specialist.

QUALIFICATIONS

There are no standard requirements for jobs in health services research careers. As with other research careers, a medical degree by itself often is sufficient; however, experience and publications in other types of research, such as outcomes research or epidemiologic research, are viewed favorably.

A master's degree or PhD can provide an advantage. A handful of graduate programs train investigators specifically in health services research, although other areas of study, such as public health, are relevant.

COMPENSATION

Given that jobs in this field span academia, government, and industry, it is difficult to narrow down a salary range. Compensation for most positions is not as high as that for clinical work.

In private sector companies funding their own studies, health services research may be only one component of a wider-ranging nonclinical job, with compensation that reflects the accompanying responsibilities.

Health Services Research Center Director

PHYSICIAN PROFILE:

Elham Hatef, MD, MPH, FACPM

JOB TITLES: Center for Population Health IT Faculty and Residency Program Academic Director

EMPLOYER: Johns Hopkins Bloomberg School of Public Health

What does your organization do?

My organization is a part of the Johns Hopkins University system and is the largest school of public health in the United States. Its mission is to protect populations through education, training, and research.

The Department of Health Policy and Management is made up of an interdisciplinary group of scholars, including scientists, health economists, and policy analysts. The department works to identify and implement policy to protect the health of populations, whether through improving access to care, financing, the organization of health care services, or the way that services are delivered.

What is your role within the organization?

I do research in the field of population health and health IT. I assess the impact of social and behavioral determinants of health on outcomes and health care utilization, using data from EHRs and sources outside the health care system, such as the U.S. Census Bureau and the American Community Survey. Such research helps health care systems to identify at-risk patients and superutilizers. It helps them design interventions to address a patient panel or people in a community who suffer from those determinants. It also helps health systems lower the cost of care for vulnerable populations. The result is improved overall health.

What are your responsibilities?

My main responsibility is leading study design. This includes identifying social and behavioral determinants with the highest impact on health outcomes and health care utilization. I then select the data sources for those variables and develop an analysis plan to assess their impact. I design implementation studies, assessing ways of using data for patient care in a health care system and on a community level.

What does a typical day on the job look like?

My day involves a lot of reading, thinking, and writing. I often work directly with the data generated within hospitals and clinics, analyzing it and considering its implications. I may attend meetings, develop presentations, and work on scientific manuscripts.

Overall, much of my day includes sitting quietly in my office, working autonomously—which I love!

How does your medical background and experience contribute to your work?

Understanding disease processes and how various social and behavioral determinants may impact health outcomes is key. Having a deep understanding of how the health care system works is imperative. This includes how health care organizations function on their own and in relation with public health agencies on a federal, state, or city level. I depend on this knowledge to design studies and disseminate information that is aligned with federal and state rules as well as ongoing initiatives in the health sector.

What are the best parts of your job?

I love the creative processes of my work and variations in foci from one project to another. I enjoy tackling major problems in the health care system and developing solutions which are evidence-based and supported by data and science.

What are the main challenges you face?

Only well-designed and well-executed studies benefit the field and effectively contribute to patient and population outcomes. A lot of thought goes into background research and planning. Data analyses don't always show what you think they will, which sometimes requires going back to the drawing board.

Additionally, working with large data sets can be challenging. It can be difficult to access data sets. There may be missing data fields, incompatible formatting, changes in collection practices over time, and variations in definitions that need to be identified and addressed to be able to use the data effectively.

Where might your career go from here?

I plan to stay in academia. I'd like to get involved in a higher level of decision-making in my health care system to assist in addressing their challenges based on the results of my research.

What are some considerations for physicians interested in a career in academia or research?

Physicians in academia need to be open to questioning themselves and their skill set. They need to constantly develop new skills. Each new project requires reading a lot of literature to figure out where we are and what the gaps are.

In health policy and health systems research, physicians need to have knowledge of public health, population health, health IT, and the health care system. They need to have some hands-on experience with data.

Most clinicians do not get training in these topics through medical school or clinical residency.

Professionals in this field, although they're in a collaborative environment, spend a lot of time working on their own. They are responsible for their own schedules. It is important to be good with time management and to be self-motivated.

The Nonprofit Sector

You're undoubtedly aware that some well-known organizations are structured as nonprofits, such as Doctors Without Borders, Compassion International, and Make-a-Wish. The fact that other organizations are nonprofits may come as a surprise—for example, the Better Business Bureau, the National Hockey League, and TED Conferences. There are over 1.5 million nonprofit organizations in the United States, and the sector is growing.[35]

From a regulatory standpoint, nonprofits are organizations with a special tax status. Functionally, they fulfill purposes that are charitable, scientific, educational, or religious, or that enhance public safety. Of workers employed by nonprofits in the United States, over half are in health-related organizations.[36]

Nonprofit organizations vary greatly in what they do and tend to have similar staffing needs as for-profit companies. Jobs in this sector have overlap with roles in other industries, but are unique in that they are mission-driven. Nonprofits measure success by their impact rather than by the profits they generate. This distinction may be critical for some physicians in selecting between nonclinical career opportunities.

Community-Serving Nonprofits and Advocacy Groups

Community-serving nonprofits make up the largest and most publicly visible component of the nonprofit sector. They include organizations that seek to increase knowledge about or awareness of certain diseases and disorders, seek to improve access to care, provide community health planning services, influence policy-making, or support patients and their families. Others provide care outside of a traditional health care delivery setting, such as at disaster or emergency sites.

Many community-serving nonprofits rely on donations for at least a portion of their budget. This isn't necessarily a setback, however. Charitable giving has been on an upward trend, with an estimated $410 billion given to charitable causes in 2017. The majority comes from individual donors.[37]

Some of the most familiar community-serving, U.S.-based nonprofits combine advocacy, education, and research into their scope of work. For example, the American Cancer Society, the Leukemia & Lymphoma Society, and the American Heart Association fit into this sector.

Some independent, private academies and research institutions operate as nonprofits to support a mission related to science or health policy. These civil associations address social and political issues that can shape the future of our economy and society.

Health foundations are nonprofit organizations that support other organizations' missions, usually by distributing funds or providing grants. The wealthiest charitable foundations in the United States include the Bill & Melinda Gates Foundation, the Howard Hughes Medical Institute, and the Robert Wood Johnson Foundation. Quasi-governmental health organizations, such as the National Science Foundation, also fit in here.

Nongovernmental organizations (NGOs) are engaged in human rights advocacy, civil development, or social activism. They effect change by exerting pressure on the public sphere. NGOs with a health focus often assume a role in which they demand accountability and transparency from the government or from industry.

THE ROLE OF NONCLINICAL PHYSICIANS

Community-serving nonprofits concentrating on health or medical topics often employ in-house functional experts, such as physicians, scientists, and public health specialists. The value of a physician within an organization depends on the focus area and scope of work.

There is no standard organizational structure among nonprofits. Each is configured to best accomplish its mission. As a result, physicians might keep one nonprofit running, whereas another nonprofit might use physicians as consultants only when their scientific expertise is needed.

Employers
- Foundation
- Health advocacy organization
- Public charity
- Social advocacy organization

The executive team is a common place for full-time physician employees in community-serving nonprofits. Many health care professionals moving into nonprofit work are drawn to the multifaceted nature of the work and the ability to wear several hats as part of a single job. There can be significant flexibility in how the work is carried out to accomplish the organization's mission.

JOB SUMMARY—DIRECTOR OF SCIENTIFIC PROGRAMS

Similar Job Titles
- Chief Medical Officer
- Director of Medical Services
- Medical Director
- Scientific Advisor

The scientific director for a community-serving nonprofit is tasked with providing leadership and strategic direction as it relates to the organization's health program or scientific research. The director provides clinical perspective, knowledge, and experience to ensure alignment between organizational goals and the output of its programs and services.

For patient advocacy groups, the scientific or medical director determines effective ways to support the patient population of interest. This may involve identifying and defining assistance programs for patients, building networks with health care providers, and supporting quality and cost management activities.

Many health-related nonprofits educate the public and health care professional communities about a particular health issue or disease. The scientific director is ultimately responsible for ensuring that any information made available is scientifically accurate and timely.

The director supports organizational research, concentrating on projects that align with trends in the medical field and directing publication and dissemination. This work may involve building relationships through discussions with key opinion leaders at scientific conferences and advisory boards.

A physician in this position serves as an information source for developments in the medical and scientific fields that may affect any aspects of the organization's work, even those that aren't directly clinical or scientific in nature, such as fundraising and marketing efforts.

Image is important to nonprofits, given their reliance on donated funds and tax-exempt status. Along with other senior staff, scientific directors develop strategies for responding to issues of public interest or media attention that relate to the organization's mission. They often have significant outward-facing responsibility, including presenting to professional audiences to aid in visibility and form partnerships.

Example Responsibilities
- Provide broad leadership and direction for scientific and clinical initiatives
- Develop and lead overall clinical or scientific vision for the organization

- Supply clinical insight for advocacy campaigns and fundraising efforts
- Advocate for legislation, infrastructure, or research within a patient population
- Ensure that programs and messaging are scientifically sound
- Provide clinical and scientific support to members of the management team
- Guide efforts to enhance research programs and ensure relevance in the scientific community
- Represent the organization at engagements within the professional community

OTHER NONCLINICAL JOB OPTIONS

Physicians with limited training or experience may be interested in jobs that do not require a medical degree, such as project director and advocacy director.

QUALIFICATIONS

Qualifications for physician leaders depend on the nonprofit's need for clinical and scientific expertise. Some positions of interest to physicians may accept candidates with any advanced scientific degree, whereas others require specialty training or a proven track record of research within a specific disease state.

Executive positions often require considerable experience in nonprofit work as well as leadership and management. Most director-level jobs involve aspects of public health and health policy, so an MPH or other public health training may be preferred.

Nonprofit organizations are driven by their missions. Candidates must wholeheartedly agree with the organization's values and vision.

COMPENSATION

Although community-serving nonprofits and advocacy groups utilize volunteers for many tasks, employees do get paid—and usually quite well. Physicians in leadership positions can expect salaries comparable to or somewhat lower than similar nonclinical positions with for-profit companies.

Because nonprofits are not profit-driven, employees don't receive profit-based bonuses.

Benefits of a community-serving nonprofit career reach beyond monetary compensation. Physicians may appreciate being able to do meaningful work and lead positive change in a health-related area they're passionate about. For some, the work is equivalent to what they'd do as a volunteer during free time. Getting paid to assist an organization that you'd consider donating your time or money to can make for a win-win situation.

Director of Scientific Programs

45. Professional Associations

Professional associations and societies aim to advance a profession and foster those who practice that profession. By pooling resources, they can accomplish a great deal that their individual members couldn't otherwise. These are member-serving nonprofits, as opposed to the community- or public-serving organizations that typically come to mind when we think of nonprofits.

Associations offer education, training, and networking opportunities. They work to spark interest among students and nurture development of early-career professionals through scholarships, mentorship, and recognition.

Acting as a collective identity and voice of a profession, associations are influential in determining acceptable practice standards and offering professional guidance. As a recognized authority in a field, an association's advocacy efforts can be geared toward the professionals themselves, regulations that affect them, their workplaces, and the patients or populations they serve.

Physicians often are active in their medical specialty or subspecialty professional associations. Other relevant associations are interdisciplinary in nature. Some are oriented toward a certain practice setting, such as telemedicine or long-term care, or focused on a functional area, such as health care quality. Organizations outside of the medical profession also are of interest to certain physicians, including pharmaceutical, managed care, and science associations.

THE ROLE OF NONCLINICAL PHYSICIANS

Many medical- and health-related professional associations have a bare-bones staff, with physician involvement limited to volunteer service through the board of directors and committees. However, some include medical professionals within the senior leadership team for the value they can offer over and above that of someone with exclusively association management experience.

Physicians know their profession firsthand and intuitively consider the professional's point of view in organizational service and advocacy efforts.

As a whole, professional associations are on the decline. Many are struggling to recruit and retain membership, because technology has made it easy to network and seek out professional resources. For physicians who are passionate about their field, a career in association management is an opportunity to influence an entire health care specialty or area of professional focus.

Employers
- Health care professional association
- Physician association or society
- Trade association

JOB SUMMARY—EXECUTIVE DIRECTOR

Similar Job Titles
- Chief Executive Officer
- Chief Operating Officer
- Executive Vice President
- President

A medical professional association executive director is responsible for driving the organization's mission through developing strategy and overseeing activities. The director is under the governance of a board of directors, which is made up of association members. The director brings issues to the board for their feedback, and the board provides input about what they see as priorities for the director.

The executive director manages staff who carry out the day-to-day association activities. Common professional association activities include offering continuing education and learning activities, organizing conferences and networking events, publishing news and scholarly work, writing position statements, political lobbying, and recruiting and retaining membership.

Relationship management is a key responsibility of an executive director. Within the organization, this involves maintaining a positive reputation among membership and the board of directors. Externally, the director works to increase the association's impact, which may involve collaborating with other organizations, meeting with professional leaders, and representing the association at events.

The executive director is an advocate and a champion for the profession. This can involve, for example, requesting that the association have representation on a committee or advisory board of a governmental or nongovernmental organization that is relevant to the profession.

Focusing on the future of the profession is important in this position. The director must ensure that the association is responsive to changes in health care trends, job market fluidity, and technological developments that may affect the field.

The association executive director role can be a challenge. Members have high expectations of what they gain from membership and what the organization accomplishes for the profession. Building revenue sources aside from membership fees can be vital to keep the association afloat. Governance can hamper the ability to act quickly. A successful director must maneuver political dynamics and tactfully modify legacy traditions.

Example Responsibilities
- Work with a board of directors to create organizational goals
- Increase the organization's visibility as an advocate and voice of the profession
- Manage a budget and produce financial reports
- Oversee revenue sources, fundraising efforts, gifts, and grants
- Develop and maintain relationships with leadership of other organizations
- Participate in national events and networking forums
- Hire and manage staff to administer the organization's range of needs
- Establish systems to engage members and increase participation
- Assist committees and task forces in association initiatives

- Establish and implement internal policies and ensure compliance with bylaws

OTHER NONCLINICAL JOB OPTIONS

Most professional association jobs suitable for physicians are executive-level roles with broad responsibility. However, large associations may have vice president–level positions that focus on a particular functional area, such as education, research, or publications.

QUALIFICATIONS

Typical association executive director qualifications are a bachelor's degree and significant experience in association leadership or nonprofit management. The requirement or preference for a medical degree is less common.

A relevant certification, such as Certified Association Executive (CAE), can enhance candidacy.

COMPENSATION

Executive professional association staff are well compensated. However, salaries vary greatly, primarily based on association size. Larger associations with more moving parts and larger budgets may offer compensation that rivals clinical work.

Executive Director

46. Certification and Accreditation

Accreditation and certification are processes by which services, programs, organizations, and individuals are evaluated to determine whether recognized performance standards are being met. These processes are commonplace in the health professions and health care services industry, as well as other fields, such as education.

In the process of accreditation, the accrediting body assesses whether a hospital or health care organization meets the minimum standards necessary to protect health and safety.

The Joint Commission, which accredits over 20,000 U.S. health care organizations, is a household name in medicine. Numerous other, less renowned bodies offer accreditation to health care organizations and programs aside from acute care hospitals. Among these are the Commission on Accreditation of Rehabilitation Facilities (CARF), American Association for Accreditation of Ambulatory Surgery Facilities (AAAASF), and the Utilization Review Accreditation Commission (URAC), to name a few.

Although the term *certification* is often used interchangeably with *accreditation*, there are differences. Entire hospitals and health care facilities are accredited. Individuals or a component of the services delivered by an organization, such as a laboratory, are certified. Certification for a health care professional indicates competence in a line of work, such as a medical specialty.

Many hospitals are motivated to seek accreditation in order to receive funding from Medicare and Medicaid programs, but the fundamental goals of accreditation surpass this. Health professions oversight helps to ensure quality of patient care. Both accreditation and certification can improve a hospital's image, increase patients' confidence in the care provided to them, attract qualified staff, and reduce costs through a focus on service efficiency and effectiveness.

THE ROLE OF NONCLINICAL PHYSICIANS

Physicians are critical to the success of accreditation and certification programs. The practice of medicine is the backbone of a health care delivery organization, and physician input ensures that the medical perspective is considered.

Standards for accreditation and certification must be sufficiently stringent. Conversely, oversight bodies have to establish requirements that applicants can reasonably achieve with the resources available to them. Physicians' experience helps to strike this balance.

During a facility's or individual's evaluation process for accreditation or certification, physicians can appropriately interpret the intent of standards and apply them to real-world situations. They can constructively discuss findings with an organization's staff and offer relevant feedback where improvement is needed.

Employers
- Accrediting or certifying body
- Medical specialty board
- Professional regulatory body
- State medical board

JOB SUMMARY—PHYSICIAN SURVEYOR

Similar Job Titles
- Lead surveyor
- Physician reviewer

A physician surveyor is involved in several aspects of the accreditation process. Working with a team of surveyors, the physician reviews information about the applicant organization and its structure and develops an approach for evaluation.

During a site visit, the surveying team employs a variety of strategies to determine whether the applicant meets the standards set in place by the accrediting body. The evaluation includes assessing the physical environment, processes used to carry out patient care, safety and emergency preparedness measures, adherence to policies, management practices, and other areas addressed in the standards.

The physician on the surveyor team is involved with the aspects of evaluation most closely related to patient care. This includes reviewing patient medical records, examining clinician training materials, and interviewing staff and patients. The surveyor needs to maintain a thorough knowledge of the accrediting body's standards and be able to apply them consistently.

Following a site visit, the surveyor documents and discusses findings with the team, which then provides explanations and recommendations to the applicant organization. The physician must provide clear rationale for any deficiencies and engage with organizational leaders to identify opportunities for improvement. Regardless of the final decision of whether to confer accreditation, a physician surveyor needs to fully support that determination in all communications.

Example Responsibilities

- Conduct evaluations of health care programs and facilities
- Determine whether accreditation standards are met
- Review patient records to analyze care delivery
- Interview clinicians, other staff, and leaders
- Analyze policies, procedures, protocols, and guidelines that affect patient care
- Document observations and report on survey findings
- Stay up to date with accreditation standards and the field of focus
- Assist in developing and writing standards and evaluation guidelines

OTHER NONCLINICAL JOB OPTIONS

There is more to an accrediting body than performing surveys. As with any business, accreditors need to have a mission and an infrastructure to remain viable. Experienced physicians with an interest in a broader role within accreditation may find that administrative positions appeal to them. These jobs might involve developing and updating accreditation standards, processes for evaluations, surveyor training activities, and educational materials for organizations seeking accreditation.

Physicians employed by medical specialty boards or other health care–certifying bodies usually occupy senior leadership positions. These include vice president or director positions, which oversee a functional area, such as assessment services or maintenance of certification.

QUALIFICATIONS

Accreditation organizations that include a physician as part of their surveyor teams typically require that the physician have recent experience in the type of health care setting that is being evaluated.

Surveyor positions require that physicians have the flexibility for frequent travel.

Qualifications for senior and executive staff for accrediting and certifying bodies vary based on their size, focus area, and specific needs. Extensive leadership or management experience may be required.

COMPENSATION

Physician surveyor positions pay, on average, slightly less than nonspecialized clinical care.

Physician Surveyor

PHYSICIAN PROFILE:

Brent R. Gibson, MD, MPH, FACPM, CAE

JOB TITLE: Chief Health Officer

EMPLOYER: National Commission on Correctional Health Care (NCCHC)

What does your organization do?

We are an umbrella 501(c)(3) with three distinct subsidiaries. The main service lines are accreditation, education, and certification. NCCHC Resources, one of the three subsidiaries, is a not-for-profit technical and management consulting firm. The other two subsidiaries are a foundation and an association management company.

What is your role within the organization?

As the organization's senior clinical executive, I work in both a leadership and technical capacity and am deeply engaged in defining the organization's overall strategy and direction. I directly advise the CEO, various NCCHC committees, and the board of directors on a variety of matters with a special emphasis on issues with clinical and public health implications.

I actively promote the commission's work by serving in numerous outreach, facilitation, and technical support capacities. I work closely with thought leaders, clinicians, and elected officials to facilitate education, training, and technical assistance as they develop local solutions for providing quality health care to incarcerated persons with specific needs.

I also serve as managing director for the affiliated not-for-profit consulting firm NCCHC Resources, Inc. Here, I provide technical assistance to correctional health care programs nationwide. I work with national health care experts on a continuous and ongoing basis to advise leaders and clinicians, monitor performance, perform auditing services, and support an overarching aim of continuous quality improvement.

What are your responsibilities?

I'm responsible for providing both knowledge and active support for sustainment and growth in the core areas of accreditation, certification, education, and publications. This is done through oversight of association activities, such as standing and ad hoc committee operations.

I am responsible for the quality assurance and quality improvement services of the NCCHC's accreditation surveys.

I advise the association's accreditation and standards committee. I act as a liaison to committees focused on juvenile health and policy and research.

As the chief health officer, I represent NCCHC at meetings of several major national organizations. These include the American Medical Association, National Institutes of Correction, and National Sheriffs' Association. I serve on committees, panels, and advisory councils within these organizations.

What does a typical day on the job look like?

I work both in the field and in the office. A typical day includes providing technical input on projects (both for clients and our own team), acquiring new business, developing and balancing project budgets, advising on strategic and government matters, leading our project management office and consultant teams, and answering questions from the field and board members.

How does your medical background and experience contribute to your work?

The job requires clinical and administrative expertise, and my background as a physician has proven essential. As an occupational medicine specialist, standards and compliance are keys to day-to-day work that translate well into the correctional environment. Furthermore, my military experience has many parallels with the corrections and law enforcement communities.

What are the best parts of your job?

I enjoy working in the strategic and big picture realm of medicine. Although I do miss seeing patients on a regular basis, working to heal vulnerable populations through strong programs is very valuable.

What are the main challenges you face?

In general, a physician in a nonclinical role is a fish out of water. No one knows what to do with you, and sometimes you are working to explain and define your role. A physician can provide tremendous value in many professional settings, but sometimes that is not apparent, even to the physician. Plus, people are always curious about why you have chosen this path over one with daily clinical responsibilities.

Where might your career go from here?

I recently passed the Certified Association Executive (CAE) exam and have taken an association executive track. The next step would be to serve as a CEO for a small association, or a senior executive for a larger association.

What are some considerations for physicians interested in a career in the nonprofit sector?

From my view, not-for-profit business is just as exciting and rewarding as for-profit business. It is true that you don't own formal interest in the entity, but, in general, your work is self-paced, you have an outsized impact on the field, and compensation can be quite reasonable if the organization is large enough. There is great opportunity to be innovative and entrepreneurial as well.

It helps to have master's-level training in health care administration, but this can be accomplished in many ways, ranging from formal degree programs to certificates. Depending on the job, training in basic business principles can be helpful as well. For me, both an MPH with a health systems administration concentration and the CAE credential have been really helpful.

Try to weave some clinical work into your career from time to time. It adds credibility and helps positively color thinking in a health care-oriented business.

Consumer Health

Consumer health refers to sectors offering a service or product to individuals who aren't patients at the point of contact. Rather, they are engaging in lifestyles to prevent disease, participating in wellness activities, working to educate themselves and self-manage disease, or planning for future health care needs.

Ease of access to information and new technologies are supporting individuals in being proactive about managing their own health. This creates a need for services that function as a bridge between health care and consumer markets.

Careers in consumer health are fitting for those who have patient care experience but are interested in assisting individuals in attaining health and maximizing their quality of life rather than in directly treating disease.

47. Health Promotion

The way we promote health has evolved with shifting disease patterns. The leading causes of death have transitioned from communicable diseases to chronic diseases, many of which are affected by lifestyle and behavioral factors, such as poor nutrition, lack of exercise, and tobacco use.

Health promotion activities are needed outside of traditional health care delivery settings to reduce the burden of chronic disease, decrease health care costs, and improve overall health.

WHO describes health promotion as the process of enabling people to increase control over their health and its determinants and thereby improve their health.[38] This can incorporate physical, mental, social, financial, and spiritual dimensions of overall health and well-being.

Employees and students spend a significant portion of their time at work and school. Consequently, workplaces and academic institutions are suitable settings to offer health promotion programs. Moreover, as technology advances, workplaces have become sedentary and simultaneously fast-paced and demanding. Programs are aimed at not only individual health but also staff retention and overall job performance.

Workplace health promotion and disease prevention programs can lower health insurance burdens for both the employer and employees. A Harvard University meta-analysis found that medical costs decrease by $3.27 for every dollar spent on a workplace health promotion program.[39]

Health and wellness coaching, often offered as a component of health promotion programs, is a market of its own. Coaching services enable individuals to improve and take charge of their health by acknowledging the need for empowerment, education, and guidance, in addition to simple instructions or a program to follow.

THE ROLE OF NONCLINICAL PHYSICIANS

Health promotion initiatives include more than annual health fairs and health classes. Physicians' understanding of the complexity of chronic disease and health determinants positions them to provide comprehensive health promotion services.

Having worked with patients in a health care setting, doctors can effectively educate individuals on medical risks and the positive effects of health behavior change. They can refer clients to medical or mental health professionals and address barriers to program participation.

Employers
- Coaching practice
- Corporation with an in-house health promotion program
- Educational institution
- Local, state, or federal government agency
- Worksite health program vendor

JOB SUMMARY—HEALTH PROGRAM DIRECTOR

Similar Job Titles
- Director of Health Promotion
- Health and Wellness Program Manager
- Health Consultant
- Health Promotion Specialist

A health program director facilitates health promotion programs that influence and assist employees at a worksite to lead healthy lifestyles. The director must identify an appropriate mix of activities and approaches to achieve program goals.

The director is essentially responsible for building a culture of health within an organization. A successful program needs to consider both employee needs and employer goals, as well as the budget, timing, and infrastructure available. New program development requires assessing baseline data, identifying opportunities for health change, and establishing measurement criteria.

Once implemented, a program may include components of health screening, health and behavior change campaigns, chronic disease management, activity tracking and incentives, team competitions and group programming, health and lifestyle coaching, and health education. Depending on the corporation's size, the director may oversee therapists, fitness instructors, nurses, coaches, and other staff.

Example Responsibilities

- Utilize data from multiple sources to identify opportunities for employee health improvement
- Consult with a client company to develop program strategy and goals
- Develop detailed project plans and work with staff to execute programming
- Use a variety of methods to promote and educate on healthy behaviors
- Evaluate health promotion strategies to determine effectiveness and impact
- Sustain a successful program by engaging in health promotion events

OTHER NONCLINICAL JOB OPTIONS

Health coaches facilitate behavior change in one-on-one or small group settings by providing direct counseling on health issues, based on client request or health assessments. Core areas of focus include physical activity, tobacco cessation, stress management, and weight management. Health coaching usually takes place in either private practice or as part of a corporate health promotion program; however, coaching firms sometimes hire full-time coaches.

Burnout, which refers to emotional exhaustion, depersonalization, and loss of satisfaction with work, is a burden to both employers and employees. It leads to decreased worker engagement, poor job satisfaction, turnover, and serious health consequences, such as depression and substance abuse. Recent attention to physician burnout by health care employers and the medical community has produced a need for peer-to-peer physician health coaching and programming aimed at preventing and addressing burnout.

QUALIFICATIONS

A career in health promotion can be a great option for physicians who are unable to obtain licensure or complete training, but who enjoy working closely with individuals on their health needs.

Experience or training in psychology, nutrition, and exercise physiology can be a plus.

COMPENSATION

Neither clinical experience nor formal medical training is required for most jobs in health promotion and, consequently, compensation can be significantly lower than that of clinical work.

However, physician health coaches may be able to command a higher salary than many coaches lacking an advanced degree.

Health Program Director

48. Case Management and Care Planning

Our health care system is complex and confusing. Disease processes and their treatments can be complex and confusing, as well. From this, several services have emerged aimed at ensuring that patients receive appropriate care in a timely manner.

Patient navigation programs assist patients and their families by coordinating appointments and specialty referrals, addressing questions and uncertainties related to their diagnosis, and consolidating medical records from multiple practices and locations. These programs most commonly are offered by hospital systems to patients with cancer or other complicated diagnoses. Nurses, social workers, and even patient peers take on the bulk of these operations.

Independent companies offering case management services have moved the patient navigation model to the next level, offering comprehensive health and wellness planning in addition to support in navigating the health care system. This highly personalized service typically requires out-of-pocket payment, and may be marketed toward affluent individuals and families who are willing to pay for customized planning, continuous access to a care team, and assistance in finding and securing appointments with specialists. Care management companies also may partner with businesses to offer their services to employees or customers.

Services in this field share the common goals of preventing care fragmentation, addressing barriers to efficient care, and improving patient satisfaction.

Case management is the implementation of services in a care plan, whereas *life care planning* is the projection of health services and their associated costs.

Life care plans are documents that provide comprehensive health-related needs and associated costs for individuals with extensive disability, injury, or illness. They are effective case management tools to be used in consultation with patients and their families, rehabilitation professionals, and others involved in carrying out the patient's health needs. They also are used in litigation to assess the impact of disability and determine the future cost of care for legal settlement purposes.

THE ROLE OF NONCLINICAL PHYSICIANS

Although a career in this field closely involves patients, a physician's role is not to diagnose and treat, but rather to manage, prevent, predict, and promote. Clinical judgment, nonetheless, is an asset in case management and care planning. Physicians are adept at understanding the implications of a diagnosis or disability, identifying appropriate service types, and effectively communicating with treating practitioners.

Life care planning is practiced by case managers, nurses, and therapists. However, these professionals—even with specialized training—rely heavily on physicians as informational sources. Although life care plans are developed as objectively as possible, they require expert opinion to draw conclusions from medical information and anticipate future medical needs.

The importance of physicians in life care planning is recognized both informally and by physician-specific certification. The physician's proficiency in analyzing medical information and formulating medical opinion improves the likelihood that a life care plan ultimately will serve its goal of improving an individual's quality of life.

Employers
- Case management company
- Insurance company
- Law firm
- Life care planning firm
- Managed care provider
- Private rehabilitation provider

JOB SUMMARY—PHYSICIAN LIFE CARE PLANNER

Similar Job Title
- Certified Life Care Planner

A physician life care planner works methodically and deliberately to develop documents that communicate an individual's care needs and accompanying costs across his or her life expectancy.

Developing a life care plan begins with a comprehensive review of medical records and supporting documentation. This is followed by patient and family interviews and a functional assessment. Contact with the patient's treatment team is often needed to fill in gaps. Review of relevant clinical practice guidelines and medical research also is conducted.

Once objective information is gathered, it is summarized and analyzed. The life care planner forms opinions about health-related services the patient may need. This requires determining likely sequelae of the patient's impairments, prognosis, and life expectancy. Some needs considered include diagnostics, physician services, medications, medical equipment and supplies, home modifications, and rehabilitation services. Finally, the expected costs of future needs and services are calculated.

Example Responsibilities
- Discuss the role of life care planning with clients
- Review medical, psychological, pharmacologic, and therapy records
- Collect and assess data related to client disability and medical needs
- Research care options and costs of care
- Use medical acumen to form opinions about future health care needs
- Participate in legal matters related to a client's life care plan

OTHER NONCLINICAL JOB OPTIONS

Case management, disability management, and complex care management companies hire medical directors to take responsibility for the clinical direction of services offered.

QUALIFICATIONS

With the exception of medical director positions, roles with care management companies do not require a medical degree or specialty training.

In life care planning roles, one of several relevant certifications is typically required. Physicians are expected to have a Certified Physician Life Care Planner designation. Physiatry training may be preferred by some organizations.

COMPENSATION

Salary figures are difficult to interpret due to the transdisciplinary nature of this field. On average, life care planner salaries are less than six figures. However, organizations specifically seeking physician life care planners are likely to pay much higher.

It is common for physician life care planners to establish their own practices or work as consultants, in which case high hourly or per-project rates are possible.

Physician Life Care Planner

49. Aesthetics, Fitness, Weight Loss, and the Wellness Industry

The wellness economy incorporates a broad range of segments. Some pick up where conventional medicine leaves off. Some are a reaction to deficiencies of a health care system focused on sickness. Others may be considered complements to medicine but, to a large extent, simply cater to our narcissism as humans.

The bulk of this sector is made up of:

- Fitness—fitness and exercise programs, equipment, and facilities.
- Nutrition—consultative services, health foods, nutraceuticals, and nutritional IV therapy.
- Weight loss—weight loss programs, diet foods, and meal services.
- Spas—day spas, stay spas, and medical spas offering cosmetic treatments and aesthetic services.
- Beauty—cosmetics, cosmeceuticals, skin and hair care, and anti-aging products.

Other types of businesses frequently included within the wellness industry are medical tourism, mind-body-spirit and holistic health practices, and components of alternative medicine.

This is a fast-paced and competitive industry in which successful companies must focus on new services and innovation to improve customer experience. It is fueled by an endless stream of trends that keep it growing. While some trends are questionable or even cringeworthy, others truly assist the consumer in achieving a state of health.

THE ROLE OF NONCLINICAL PHYSICIANS

Physicians have a clear place in certain aspects of the aesthetics industry. Injections and laser treatments provided at medical spas, for example, involve the practice of medicine. Although services routinely are delegated to nurses, aestheticians, and other licensed staff, physicians are ultimately responsible and are held to the same standards as in conventional medicine.

Similarly, weight-loss programs that incorporate prescription medications are medical practices that require physician oversight.

In this sense, many physician positions with these companies are not technically nonclinical; however, many have minimal clinical responsibility. Patient interaction often is limited to healthy clients seeking elective services.

Offering wellness commodities that effectively serve their purpose and satisfy consumers requires knowledge of physiology, metabolism, and anatomy in the healthy body. When consumers aren't already healthy, physician experience and knowledge of pathophysiology comes into play.

The rise of medical fitness facilities is a great example of the need for physicians in this sector. Traditional fitness centers cater to the young and healthy, but there is increasing interest in tailoring services toward older adults and those with illness and disabilities. There also is a trend for health clubs to partner with physician practices and include active medical oversight and clinical integration of their programs.

Employers
- Aesthetics practice
- Fitness or training center
- Medical fitness facility
- Medical spa

JOB SUMMARY—MEDICAL DIRECTOR

An administrative medical director has a similar role across a range of businesses in the wellness industry, including medical spas, medical weight loss centers, and medical fitness facilities. The medical director has overall responsibility for the clinical and medical aspects of the business. This consists of developing relevant policies and procedures, training clinical staff, reviewing documentation, and ensuring quality of services. The director may be used in a consultative capacity for human resources, legal, operational, and marketing matters.

Attracting and retaining clients in this industry can be a challenge. Medical directors may be involved in selecting and developing new lines of business based on trends in the industry, client feedback, and regulatory changes.

Example Responsibilities

- Oversee the activity and training of all clinical personnel
- Provide supervision of medical and health-related programs and services
- Review documentation and conduct peer reviews and clinical audits
- Assess client suitably for various programs, procedures, and treatments
- Develop relationships with vendors to maximize service profitability and efficiency
- Keep informed of developments and trends in the field to guide business decisions
- Research and recommend new services or changes to existing services
- Maintain knowledge of state and federal regulations related to services

It is more common for physicians to be either owners or consultants than full-time employees of medical spas and similar wellness businesses. Practices in which procedures can be performed by nurses or aestheticians may not need a physician on a full-time basis. Moreover, some states prohibit what is known as the "corporate practice of medicine," generally meaning that non-physicians cannot own medical practices.

OTHER NONCLINICAL JOB OPTIONS

Nutraceutical, cosmeceutical, and other wellness product companies hire physicians for product development and scientific affairs positions.

For physicians who are unable to obtain a medical license, their clinical background can be an asset for wellness industry positions that typically do not require a medical degree. Innovative fitness centers, for example, are offering the expertise of highly trained professionals to clients seeking to "train like an athlete" or reach their performance peaks.

Finally, there are opportunities for physicians to bridge the gap between the medical industry and various sectors of the wellness industry through partnerships between medical and wellness practices and through conducting rigorous scientific research.

QUALIFICATIONS

Most treatments and procedures offered at medical spas and other wellness practices require an active license but not board certification. Positions that do not involve medical procedures or prescribing have less stringent qualifications.

COMPENSATION

Compensation varies greatly depending on the company and the role. Physicians must get creative to find a job in this field that is as lucrative as clinical work. This could be done by taking a leadership position at a wellness company with a novel business model or working with a company to implement new revenue sources.

Administrative Medical Director

50. Broadcast Media and Entertainment

Broadcast media, such as radio and television, plays a major—and, at times, critical—part in Americans' lives. It is consumed deliberately to stay informed of current events and as a form of enjoyment and education. It also comes at us passively during everyday activities, such as entering a store with the radio playing or sitting in a waiting room with a television.

Although few physicians have careers within media and entertainment, the range of pathways to potentially land in this field is considerable. There are opportunities in news broadcasting, TV entertainment, film, and even broadcast advertising.

THE ROLE OF NONCLINICAL PHYSICIANS

Television has undergone significant change in recent years, becoming interactive, digitized, and customized for viewers. There has been consolidation in the industry. Many commercial television stations are now owned by large media conglomerates, with many owning several network affiliates. Physician expertise is valuable for medical news and for programming on niche networks to avoid bias and ensure quality.

Physicians are needed to identify the relevant aspects of health-related news, put that news in context, and present it in a way that is understandable and relatable to viewers. Moreover, on-air medical professionals bring credibility to medical news. This is particularly important in the case of disease outbreaks or other urgent situations in which broadcast media is the most efficient way to distribute information to the general public.

Medical experience is needed to ensure accuracy and relevance of medical and health information in educational programming as well as medical dramas and reality series.

Finally, physicians' ease of networking in the medical community can simplify the process of securing experts for interviews.

Employers
- Entertainment company
- Television network

JOB SUMMARY—MEDICAL CORRESPONDENT

Similar Job Titles
- On-Air Health Expert
- Medical Consultant
- Health Correspondent

Medical correspondents help to present news that digs deeper than the surface details, delivering clinical expertise or a medical angle. In some cases, they provide explanation for complex medical stories. In others, they provide depth and significance to an otherwise simple story.

A correspondent's work starts with analyzing a story and researching any relevant data or studies. Correspondents work with a team to plan shows or portions of shows, such as a medical "beat." On air, a medical correspondent is tasked with presenting the news in a professional yet entertaining way. This can involve both scripted and ad lib material as well as interviews. It may be delivered in a newsroom or from the field.

Medical correspondents may respond urgently to breaking medical news and make public appearances on behalf of the station.

Example Responsibilities
- Deliver news on-air with confidence, enthusiasm, and competence
- Assist in the research, writing, and coordination of programming
- Provide expertise to add depth to medical and health news
- Put medical news into context with relevant data and research
- Apply and adapt programming and delivery elements based on audience analysis
- Find sources, maintain contacts, and pursue leads for original stories
- Maintain familiarity of medical and health issues and current events of interest to the network

OTHER NONCLINICAL JOB OPTIONS

Off-air jobs for physicians also exist in television. Medical producers are employed by networks that routinely air medical content. A producer is involved in the full scope of production, including researching, planning interviews and visual elements, and writing content. Depending on the organization's needs, a producer may be focused on a single TV series or may be involved in producing medical material across multiple outlets operated by the network. Other relevant job titles include Medical Unit Director, Chief Medical Expert, and Medical Division Manager.

Careers as TV writers, screenwriters, and in advertising media also are possibilities.

QUALIFICATIONS

Media and entertainment is a difficult field to break into. For some physicians, it requires essentially taking a demotion. Others may achieve success quickly through a combination of expertise, ability to entertain, and being in the right place at the right time to be "discovered."

Those who find success in broadcast media go where the jobs are—primarily the largest U.S. cities, such as New York and Los Angeles.

For on-air positions, the ability to perform and entertain in front of the camera goes a long way.

COMPENSATION

Compensation varies greatly by experience and market size. Few people make serious money in entertainment right off the bat. This is a field in which your passion must carry you.

Medical Correspondent

Michael Crupain, MD, MPH

JOB TITLE: Medical Unit Chief of Staff

EMPLOYER: The Doctor Oz Show

What does your organization do?

The Doctor Oz Show is the leading daytime television program about health.

What is your role within the organization?

I am essentially the medical director for the show. My team helps shape the health content of what appears on both the show and its associated outlets. We work to ensure that it is both helpful to our audience and accurate.

What are your responsibilities?

I manage a team of medical researchers who work with producers to shape the show's health content and confirm its accuracy. I ensure that investigations and lab testing are done using proper methodology. I oversee the creation of medical graphics and animations. I produce content not only for the show but also for the website, social media, and external publications.

I manage external relations on behalf of the organization with medical groups and federal and local health agencies. I run any public health campaigns that the organization is engaged in. I work with the public relations and affiliates department to ensure that Dr. Oz has accurate talking points for interviews or segments on other shows (for example, *The Today Show*).

What does a typical day on the job look like?

There are really no average days at the *Doctor Oz Show*! Some typical things I might do in a day could be: attend a briefing with Dr. Oz to get him ready for the show, meet with producers to discuss a segment idea, have a phone call with the Surgeon General's office to discuss an initiative, review transcript notes from my staff, write an article about new cancer screening guidelines, read scripts, review social media posts, and go over an animation with the graphics team.

How does your medical background and experience contribute to your work?

My medical training—especially my residency in preventive medicine—greatly benefits the work I do every day. I need to have a good background on a wide variety of health and public health topics as well as a strong understanding of research methodology, anatomy, clinical practice guidelines, the organization of health systems, and how policy and environmental issues impact health.

What are the best parts of your job?

My personal mission in life is to make the world a healthier place. The media has the power to impact millions of lives at a time. It can influence individual behavior as well as our culture.

What are the main challenges you face?

One of the biggest challenges is learning how to talk to "regular people" about medical topics. As good as you may think you are at it, you can always be better. In a doctor's office, it's rare that a patient asks questions to the point that they truly understand what we're explaining to them, so we don't have a good opportunity to hone these skills. In television, you have to really learn how to translate medicine into a language that can be instantly understood.

Where might your career go from here?

I never know where my career is going to go next. I'm always looking for new opportunities where I can have a bigger impact. I recently co-wrote a book called *What to Eat When* with Dr. Michael Roizen, which led me to the front of the camera to talk about it. My next move will probably be to work in an organization that creates media and combines it with new innovative ways to improve population health.

What are some considerations for physicians interested in a career in media or entertainment?

To work in the media, you should be creative, be a team player, be a good negotiator, enjoy working at a fast pace, and accept uncertainty and frequent change. You must have a strong desire to learn how to translate medical concepts into a language that your audience understands.

I've been very fortunate in my career to have unique media jobs, first at Consumer Reports and then at *The Doctor Oz Show*. These are really one-of-a-kind opportunities. There aren't enough positions for many physicians to work full-time in the media. With that in mind, there are great opportunities and I encourage people with a passion for media to seek them out.

Bonus! Independent Physician Consulting and Entrepreneurship

Physicians in full-time, employed nonclinical positions enjoy a reliable paycheck and well-defined role. They receive benefits, sensible work hours, and opportunities for promotion and lateral career moves.

There are drawbacks to this type of employment, though. Salaries are limited. You must do the work your employer asks you to do. You have to follow the rules. You might not like your coworkers or the office culture.

Working for yourself or starting a business means that you call the shots (within the confines of the law). There is no ceiling on what you can earn. Your business could potentially have a huge impact on a field, a market, or a segment of the population.

These are a few reasons that many nonclinical physicians opt for self-employment.

INDEPENDENT CONSULTING

Independent consultants are hired for many reasons. Consultants are brought on board to help create a new business, bring about change in an existing business, identify problems, deliver objectivity, or act as a catalyst. A theme throughout all areas of independent consulting is providing expertise to solve a problem or meet a demand.

In most cases, physician consulting clients are businesses. Common types include:

- Expert witness services
- High-level strategy for health care companies
- Medical chart review
- Medical practice technology implementation

- Medical writing
- Speaking engagements

Other consulting services are aimed at individuals, such as:

- Career coaching
- Personalized weight loss and fitness services
- Tutoring

There are many niches for physician consultants. A doctor with a research background can offer publication planning services. Prior success in marketing a medical practice can situate a physician to advise on digital marketing strategies for others' practices. Physicians with experience in pharmacoepidemiology may find success in performing drug safety case reviews.

Setting up a consulting practice begins by recognizing an area of expertise and identifying a need within a target market.

ENTREPRENEURSHIP

There are countless examples of successful physician entrepreneurs. Our intelligence, motivation, and curiosity prepare us well for entrepreneurship. What is lacking for many physicians is business acumen; however, this can be learned through self-study, earning an MBA, working with a startup, or even trial and error.

Businesses that tend to have the lowest barriers to entry are service businesses. These can offer a service directly to consumers, to other businesses, or through a software or technology solution. Independent physician consultants with more work than they can handle single-handedly can hire employees and transition from a solo consultant to a CEO.

Physical, tangible products are another opportunity for physician entrepreneurs. Bringing a product to market requires additional time and upfront investment compared with getting a service business off the ground. Additionally, there can be substantial risk and regulatory hurdles—especially for medical products. Nonetheless, product-based businesses are scalable, potentially disruptive of existing markets, and can be financially rewarding.

Medicine is a fitting foundation for a breadth of nonclinical business types. The world is your oyster, the sky is the limit, and all those clichés.

Transitioning to a Nonclinical Job

Gaining an appreciation for the types of nonclinical jobs available to physicians is a solid first step in transitioning a career. But several steps stand between this and landing a new job. Although it is not a comprehensive guide to a nonclinical job search, the following section intends to provide considerations for selecting a path, identifying job opportunities, and effectively transitioning a career from clinical to nonclinical.

SELECTING BETWEEN NONCLINICAL JOB TYPES

The 50 chapters on nonclinical careers demonstrate the breadth of industries and business areas that are available to physicians. The goal was to be informative if you were seeking direction, inspiring if your career has become lifeless, and liberating if you were concerned that a nonclinical career might be confining.

COMPARING JOB TYPES ACROSS MULTIPLE INDUSTRIES

Simply being aware of the options does not inevitably discern which career option is the best one for you to pursue. Multiple job types across different sectors can be both fitting and attainable. It can be helpful to consider nonclinical jobs not just by industry, but by the extent to which clinical skills and experience are necessary to excel at the job.

Nonclinical jobs can be roughly split into categories based on their degree of separation from clinical medicine. Clinical knowledge and proficiency may be:

- Crucial and required
- Directly advantageous
- Indirectly, yet significantly, pertinent
- Unnecessary but generally applicable
- Influential, though minimally relevant

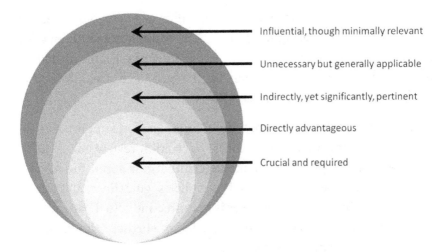

Influential, though minimally relevant

Unnecessary but generally applicable

Indirectly, yet significantly, pertinent

Directly advantageous

Crucial and required

JOBS IN WHICH CLINICAL PROFICIENCY IS CRUCIAL AND REQUIRED

Careers in this category require active provider-level medical decision-making or advising. These jobs are as close to practicing medicine as you can get without actually spending each day seeing a panel of patients.

Jobs of this nature often are with companies that offer clinical services to patients, such as hospitals or health care systems. Nonclinical physicians with this type of career can be in leadership positions in which they guide other clinicians in the processes and policies used in caring for patients. Sometimes, the work may require getting so closely involved with patient care that an active license is required. Examples include a health care system CMO or a health services company corporate medical director.

Work in which clinical proficiency is crucial also can take place outside of a health care delivery setting, yet rely on a deep understanding of medicine and on extensive experience in treating patients within a medical subfield. Physicians working in medical law fall into this category.

JOBS IN WHICH CLINICAL PROFICIENCY IS DIRECTLY ADVANTAGEOUS

Many nonclinical jobs unequivocally depend on a physician's clinical skills and experience for carrying out responsibilities, but those responsibilities do not directly affect the care that a patient receives.

As with the previous category, these jobs often are with companies that are involved in delivering health care. The work, however, is an additional step removed from actual patient care. A physician with a job of this kind in a hospital setting may be involved in clinical informatics, quality improvement, or medical affairs.

Other careers of this type are with companies that support medical organizations through their services. Utilization review, for instance, requires that the physician make determinations about the medical necessity of clinical services based on policies, guidelines, and clinical evidence. In this case, the reviewer is not directing actual patient treatment, but, rather, is making a decision about whether the services will be covered by the patient's insurance.

Other positions in which clinical proficiency is directly advantageous include managed care medical director, CMIO, and physician advisor.

JOBS IN WHICH CLINICAL PROFICIENCY IS INDIRECTLY, YET SIGNIFICANTLY, PERTINENT

Some nonclinical roles benefit heavily from clinical knowledge and experience, but the benefit is indirect. Physicians in this type of job often work to develop or implement a product or solution that ultimately will be used by or benefit a hospital or medical practice.

The product or solution could be a drug or health tech device, for example. It is immensely helpful to have firsthand experience in the end user's shoes for decisions related to the product design, as well as strategy for marketing it, implementing it, and measuring its impact.

Any considerations about patient care in this type of nonclinical job tend to be on a population or market level. Physicians might consider the unmet health care needs of an entire patient demographic or the educational needs of physician specialists who will prescribe a new drug.

JOBS IN WHICH CLINICAL PROFICIENCY IS UNNECESSARY BUT GENERALLY APPLICABLE

Many nonclinical careers allow physicians to make use of their comprehensive clinical knowledge and experience without depending on it.

Physicians working in management consulting often are assigned to projects with health care systems or medical product companies as the client. The goal of the project may be to make a recommendation about a merger or other high-level business decision. However, considerations made in developing that recommendation can be strengthened by understanding clinically related factors, such as how a service affects patient health. This is one of the reasons that consulting firms hire physicians.

Medical writing is another example of this career type. Although adept medical writers may have only a bachelor's degree, they do not have the deep-seated medical knowledge or field experience of a medical writer with an MD. This gives physicians a boost in landing more senior medical writing positions and higher salaries.

Although work of this type is only tangentially related to medical practice, physicians will feel that they're actively making use of their extensive training for certain job tasks.

JOBS IN WHICH CLINICAL PROFICIENCY IS INFLUENTIAL, THOUGH MINIMALLY RELEVANT

Finally, it is worth noting that clinical experience is influential even for physicians who choose to transition their careers to work that is unrelated to medicine or health.

Physicians working in real estate might consider the health of a population in a geographic area or a property's proximity to adequate medical care. Or they might employ their medical knowledge to invest in medical office buildings.

A physician who opens a bakery has a leg up over a pastry chef in considering how health needs and diet trends can make their way into the business model.

A physician turning a passion for fine art into a full-time career may be inspired by prior patient encounters.

CONSIDER YOUR SKILLS BROADLY

Just as clinical experience is never useless to a nonclinical career, other skills gained from clinical work are assets to jobs outside of patient management.

Physicians considering nonclinical work often feel that they're not adequately prepared or are lacking the appropriate skill set. New skills and knowledge undoubtedly will be needed. This is true of any job change. However, some skills naturally acquired from training and working in medicine that may seem unrelated to nonclinical work on the surface are actually quite relevant. Here are several:

- **Asking the right questions.** We know how to ask the right questions to obtain the information we need or get to the heart of a problem. Physicians do this with patients at every encounter. In a nonclinical setting, the same concept applies to clients, coworkers, and customers.
- **Self-teaching and keeping up with changes in a field.** Biomedical research, clinical guidelines, and even Medicare rules are constantly changing and published at a rapid pace. To practice effectively, physicians can never stop learning. Success in many nonclinical roles relies on the ability to learn new information and keep abreast of trends in the field.
- **Rolling with the punches.** Physicians have disagreements with colleagues. We request payments for medical services that are denied by insurance companies. We get sued. We deal with countless frustrations. Nonclinical jobs come with punches, as well. Physicians are prepared to roll with them.
- **Pleasing multiple stakeholders.** Clinical work would be simpler if we had only our patients to consider. But we contend with insurance companies, hospital systems, accreditors, and patients' family members. In nonclinical work, the stakeholders may be boards of directors, advocacy groups, funding agencies, elected officials, clients, and the media.
- **Delegating work.** We do a lot ourselves as doctors, but we delegate a lot, as well. On an inpatient unit, providers delegate work to nurses, ancillary service staff, administrative assistants, students, and case managers. Nonclinical physicians often are in positions in which proficient delegating is needed for success.
- **Managing time effectively.** Every physician knows the feeling of having an overwhelming amount to do in one day. We've learned how to get it done by prioritizing and using time productively. Our ability

to effectively manage time, although it may have been learned during our time on the wards, is not restricted to patient care.

- **Being reliable and taking responsibility.** We need to be reliable when caring for patients. Lives are at stake. We take responsibility and follow through with what we say we're going to do. This skill is surprisingly lacking in the workforce as a whole, so it is an area in which nonclinical physicians can stand out.
- **Knowing your limits.** We've learned to avoid trying to be heroes. We know when to tell a patient that their disease is too complex for us to manage alone. We know when to consult a colleague, when to try a different approach, and when to call a death during a code. A nonclinical career may put you in the midst of large, complicated projects. Without knowing your limits and knowing when to ask for help, you can work furiously without making headway.

Moving from clinical medicine to a nonclinical career is a big change, for sure. But we all have an extensive toolbox of skills. They can be used as selling points during a job search, to carry us through the first few months on a new job, and to advance our nonclinical careers.

EXPERIENCE WHEN YOU HAVE NO EXPERIENCE

As with skills, work experience must be considered broadly for physicians applying to nonclinical jobs. Many industry job listings indicate that a certain amount of experience within the industry is required. In some cases, this requirement can be disregarded when sending in an application. If the job otherwise sounds like a good fit for you, apply anyway.

When applying to a job in an industry in which you have no experience, highlight relevant professional activities in your resume and cover letter. For example, an application for a position in pharmacovigilance benefits from emphasizing involvement in clinical research studies or serving on a hospital's pharmacy and therapeutics committee.

A cover letter is an excellent place to explain what your professional experience has entailed. It can be used to justify how your experience fits with the job requirements. A recruiter may not draw connections between the experience listed on your resume and the position being filled. But you can draw these connections for the recruiter. By doing so, you greatly increase the chances that your resume will be passed on to the hiring manager.

TIMING YOUR TRANSITION

Deciding when to transition to a nonclinical career can be a tough decision. It is also a highly personal decision. There is no right or wrong time to do it.

One piece of advice that is applicable to every physician's decision is this: don't act out of frustration.

Many physicians begin to think about nonclinical roles when they are dissatisfied with their work or burned out in clinical medicine. These feelings should not be the main drivers of switching to nonclinical work. Transition to a nonclinical job because you want the job and because it represents a step forward in meeting your personal and professional goals.

TAKING A LEAP VERSUS TAKING STEPS TOWARD A NONCLINICAL CAREER

Physicians who are not sure whether nonclinical work is the right decision can find some clarity by dipping a toe in the water. Taking on administrative duties at your hospital or clinical practice is an option for those interested in nonclinical jobs in health care delivery settings.

Some companies hire physicians as part-time contractors. This is common in utilization management, disability insurance, and other types of chart review work. Freelance opportunities are available in several areas of medical writing. Startup companies without the budget or need for a full-time medical director may bring in physicians on a contracted basis. Universities hire adjunct faculty to teach as little as one course per semester. These are just a few possible ways to get a feel for whether a transition to a certain nonclinical career is the right choice.

Starting nonclinical work doesn't need to be an "all or nothing" change. For many doctors who have grown accustomed to practicing clinically, the thought of transitioning to a nonclinical job is as terrifying as it is exciting. Making a transition gradually can ease anxiety as well as make it easier to revert back to full-time clinical work if a nonclinical career doesn't turn out to be a good fit.

COMPLETING A RESIDENCY

Some doctors begin leaning toward a nonclinical career before finishing residency, or even during medical school. In these cases, a decision must be made about whether to complete residency prior to taking a nonclinical job.

The long hours, low pay, and unenjoyable aspects of residency can make a nonclinical job sound appealing. The thought of doing years of extra clinical work while knowing you ultimately do not want to be a clinician is an exhausting thought. In almost all cases, though, the advantages of completing a residency outweigh the downsides.

Clinical work in a care-directive capacity is one of the few things that truly sets physicians apart from other professionals. Gaining clinical experience prior to transitioning to a nonclinical career will expand the possibilities available to you.

Having a board certification recognized by the American Board of Medical Specialties or the American Osteopathic Association is a requirement for a large percentage of well-compensated nonclinical jobs. Even when it is not required, it is often considered a plus for the applicant. The extra three to six years of training imparts substantial skills and knowledge that are valuable for many nonclinical jobs. Moreover, board certification garners respect for nonclinical roles involving collaboration with other medical professionals.

KEEPING UP YOUR CLINICAL SKILLS (OR NOT)

Whether to continue working clinically after transitioning to a nonclinical job depends on personal circumstances.

The logistics for continuing to practice clinically vary between nonclinical jobs. Some employers allow physicians in nonclinical positions to spend a portion of their time out of the office seeing patients. This might be a half day per week, a few full days per month, or another arrangement. The schedule sometimes is negotiable.

It is advantageous to continue practicing clinically in some capacity for several reasons. First, it can be tough to reenter clinical medicine if you've gone a long time without practicing. Even if you think you'll never want to go back to a clinical job, we all change our minds on occasion. Our situations change, our interests evolve, and our priorities switch directions. By continuing clinical work, you may be able to better accommodate these life changes.

Second, clinical work legitimizes you, especially among other doctors. There's a good chance you'll be interacting with medical professionals in your nonclinical role. If you are still treating patients, other physicians may find it easier to communicate with you, feel that you understand them, and believe that you can empathize with their pain points.

Ongoing clinical work can make it easier to change positions—even to other nonclinical jobs. Many nonclinical jobs require the applicant to have a certain amount of recent clinical experience. The type and setting may not even matter. The fact that it is recent and uninterrupted tends to be more important.

Finally, clinical work can be a significant source of extra income. Patient care often pays better than nonclinical work on an hourly basis. The pay from even a single moonlighting shift each week can really add up.

On the other hand, continuing part-time or intermittent clinical work may not be feasible, desirable, or beneficial for some doctors. Those who truly do not enjoy any type of clinical practice may be better off focusing entirely on nonclinical activities. Patient care may be of little value to physicians nearing retirement or those who are confident they will never return to clinical medicine. With some full-time nonclinical jobs, the logistical challenge of fitting in clinical work might be excessive. Lastly, some physicians are physically unable to perform the duties of clinical work or are unable to obtain a medical license.

TRANSFERRING BETWEEN SECTORS AND INDUSTRIES

Nonclinical doctors can pivot from managed care to hospital administration, from a federal agency to management consulting, from medical writing to pharmaceutical medical affairs, and in countless other ways.

A mentor of mine once described her career as "meandering." This word has stuck with me as I've made decisions about my own nonclinical career.

Thanks to the significant overlap between physician roles in many types of nonclinical medicine, beginning a nonclinical job does not tie you to a specific industry or line of work. Additionally, working your way "up the corporate ladder" has fallen out of fashion across the general workforce. Strong organizations value a candidate's experience in different fields and position types. It stimulates innovation and gives a fresh perspective to the way things are done.

Physicians in any type of practice are leaders. This is rooted in our profession. Naturally, nonclinical roles for physicians tend to be leadership positions, as well. The leadership components of some nonclinical jobs—such as CMO—are obvious, whereas others are more subtle. A utilization management physician who primarily works independently to evaluate prior authorization requests is still considered a leader within a multidisciplinary reviewer team, for instance.

Leadership proficiency is a cross-discipline skill. It takes more time and more effort to learn to be a good leader than it does to learn the details and nuances of an industry such as health insurance or medical devices. For this reason, physicians are especially well-suited to transition between nonclinical roles in different sectors.

Conclusion: Where to Go From Here

You're equipped now with the knowledge of 50 nonclinical career opportunities. Where to go from here depends on your own goals and timeline.

Networking and mentorship are universally valuable for nonclinical jobseekers. Surround yourself with physicians who are supportive and inspirational.

It can feel isolating to be in a clinical setting while looking into nonclinical jobs, especially for physicians whose colleagues are passionate about clinical work. That isolation can be prevented by having a mentor (or several mentors) to support you in your journey. Establish relationships with physicians in roles that you aspire to have. Keep in touch with former teachers and coworkers who took a similar path to a nonclinical job. These connections will offer guidance and help you feel confident in the decisions you make.

Professional societies and associations are excellent resources for physicians interested in nonclinical careers. Membership often includes mentorship programs, career resources, educational materials, and networking opportunities.

By developing and growing your connections, you can guarantee that you'll always have someone to answer your questions, provide advice, or introduce you to someone else who can help.

THE FUTURE OF NONCLINICAL MEDICINE

There is a demand for nonclinical physicians, and the demand is growing. This is due, in part, to the growth of industries that depend on medical and clinical expertise, including health IT, digital health, pharmaceuticals, and managed care. New technologies and approaches to health care will expand nonclinical options down the road.

Nevertheless, competition for certain nonclinical jobs will intensify over time. According to a 2016 survey of more than 17,000 U.S. physicians, 13.5% plan to seek a nonclinical job within the next three years, which is increased from prior year surveys.[40] Over half of U.S. physicians are experiencing symptoms of professional burnout,[41] a key motivator for considering nonclinical work.

To remain a competitive candidate, you should stay up to date with advances in the science of medicine while embracing opportunities to master new skills, become a competent leader, and develop business acumen.

References

1. Pharmaceutical Research and Manufacturers of America. 2019 PhRMA Annual Membership Survey. https://www.phrma.org/-/media/Project/PhRMA/PhRMA-Org/PhRMA-Org/PDF/P-R/PhRMA_2019_membership_survey_Final.pdf

2. Q4 2018 Venture Monitor. *PitchBook–National Venture Capital Association.* January 9, 2019. https://pitchbook.com/news/reports/4q-2018-pitchbook-nvca-venture-monitor.

3. Department of Health and Human Services. FY 2020 Budget-in-Brief. www.hhs.gov/sites/default/files/fy-2020-budget-in-brief.pdf

4. Association of American Medical Colleges. *The Complexities of Physician Supply and Demand: Projections from 2017 to 2032.* April 2019. https://aamc-black.global.ssl.fastly.net/production/media/filer_public/31/13/3113ee5c-a038-4c16-89af-294a69826650/2019_update_-_the_complexities_of_physician_supply_and_demand_-_projections_from_2017-2032.pdf

5. Ibid.

6. O'Reilly KB. New medical schools open but physician shortage concerns persist. *amednews.com.* March 29, 2010. https://amednews.com/article/20100329/profession/303299963/2/.

7. American Community Survey. Public Use Microdata Samples. United States Census Bureau. 2017. https://www.census.gov/programs-surveys/acs/data/pums.html

8. Medscape Physician Compensation Report – 2019. https://www.medscape.com/slideshow/2019-compensation-overview-6011286

9. athenahealth analysis of data from the Bureau of Labor Statistics, the National Center for Health Statistics, and the United States Census Bureau's Current Population Survey. https://www.athenahealth.com/insight/expert-forum-rise-and-rise-healthcare-administrator

10. Woolhandler S, Himmelstein DU. The deteriorating administrative efficiency of the US health care system. *N Engl J Med.* 1991;324:1253-1258.

11. 2018 U.S. HIMSS Leadership and Workforce Survey. https://www.himss.org/sites/hde/files/d7/u132196/2018_HIMSS_US_LEADERSHIP_WORKFORCE_SURVEY_Final_Report.pdf

12. Cejka Executive Search. Physician Leadership Compensation Survey. 2016.

13. Corrigan JM. Crossing the quality chasm. Building a better delivery system. February 27, 2005. https://www.ncbi.nlm.nih.gov/books/NBK22849/

14. PhRMA. *Biopharmaceutical R & D: The Process Behind New Medicines.* 2015. www.phrma.org/Report/Biopharmaceutical-R-and-D-The-Process-Behind-New-Medicines

15. Office of the Press Secretary. Fact sheet: At cancer moonshot summit, Vice President Biden Announces new actions to accelerate progress toward ending cancer as we know it. *Whitehouse.gov.* June 28, 2016. www.whitehouse.gov/the-press-office/2016/06/28/fact-sheet-cancer-moonshot-summit-vice-president-biden-announces-new.

16. Office of the Press Secretary. Fact sheet: President Obama's precision medicine initiative. *Whitehouse.gov.* January 30, 2015. https://www.whitehouse.gov/the-press-office/2015/01/30/fact-sheet-president-obama-s-precision-medicine-initiative.

17. Notsa J. Digital health for dummies. *Forbes.* May 19, 2013. https://www.forbes.com/sites/johnnosta/2013/05/19/digital-health-for-dummies/#d0d571b7a1cd

18. Insurance Information Institute, Inc. Facts + Statistics: Industry Overview. https://www.iii.org/fact-statistic/facts-statistics-industry-overview.

19. Okoro CA, Hollis ND, Cyrus AC, Griffin-Blake S. Prevalence of disabilities and health care access by disability status and type among adults — United States, 2016. *MMWR Morb Mortal Wkly Rep.* 2018;67:882-887. www.cdc.gov/mmwr/volumes/67/wr/mm6732a3.htm

20. Persons with a disability: labor force characteristics – 2018. News Release. Bureau of Labor Statistics. February 26, 2019. www.bls.gov/news.release/pdf/disabl.pdf.

21. IQVIA. *The National Economic Impact of Physicians: National Report.* January 2018. www.ama-assn.org/sites/ama-assn.org/files/corp/media-browser/public/2018-ama-economic-impact-study.pdf

22. Executive Talent 2020. Association of Executive Search and Leadership Consultants. www.aesc.org/sites/default/files/uploads/magazine/Executive_Talent_Magazine_issue7.pdf

23. Science and the Media Expert Group. Science and the Media: Securing the Future. January 2010. www.sciencemediacentre.org/wp-content/uploads/2010/01/Science-and-the-Media-Expert-Group-Securing-the-Future.pdf.

24. Lifson SS. Health education in industry – practical considerations for actual programs in industry. *Am J Public Health Nations Health.* 1959;49:1357-1363.

25. FDA at a glance. US Food and Drug Administration. August 2018. www.fda.gov/media/115824/download.

26. Bureau of Labor Statistics. The employment situation—December 2019. www.bls.gov/news.release/pdf/empsit.pdf 27. Bureau of Labor Statistics. American Time Use Survey. 2017. https://www.bls.gov/news.release/archives/atus_06282018.pdf

28. Easton D. *The Political System: An Inquiry Into the State of Political Science.* New York: Knopf; 1953. www.jstor.org/stable/pdf/2126540

29. The Henry J. Kaiser Family Foundation. Professionally Active Physicians. March 2019. www.kff.org/other/state-indicator/total-active-physicians

30. Glaze LE, Kaeble D. U.S. Department of Justice. Office of Justice Programs. Bureau of Justice Statistics. Correctional populations in the United States. 2013. www.bjs. gov/content/pub/pdf/cpus13.pdf

31. CareerCast.com. The least stressful jobs of 2018. www.careercast.com/ jobs-rated/2018-least-stressful-jobs.

32. National Institutes of Health. What we do: budget. 2019. www.nih.gov/about-nih/ what-we-do/budget.

33. Lohr KN, Steinwachs DM. Health services research: an evolving definition of the field. *Health Serv Res*. 2002;37(1):7-9. https://www.ncbi.nlm.nih.gov/pmc/articles/ PMC1430351/.

34. Coalition for Health Services Research. *Federal Funding for Health Services Research*. Washington, DC: 2009.

35. McKeever B. The nonprofit sector in brief. *Urban Institute*. August 28, 2018. https:// nccs.urban.org/project/nonprofit-sector-brief

36. Salamon LM, Sokolowski SW, Haddock MA, Tice HS. *The State of Global Civil Society and Volunteering*. Comparative Nonprofit Sector Working Paper No. 49. Center for Civil Society Studies, 2012. http://ccss.jhu.edu/wp-content/uploads/ downloads/2013/04/JHU_Global-Civil-Society-Volunteering_FINAL_3.2013.pdf

37. *Giving USA 2018: The Annual Report on Philanthropy for the Year 2017*. Chicago: Giving USA Foundation.

38. World Health Organization. *The Bangkok Charter for Health Promotion in a Globalized World*. Geneva, Switzerland: WHO, 2005. https://www.who.int/ healthpromotion/conferences/6gchp/bangkok_charter/en/

39. Baicker K, Cutler D, Song Z. Workplace wellness programs can generate savings. *Health Aff (Millwood)*. 2010;29:304-311. https://www.healthaffairs.org/doi/10.1377/ hlthaff.2009.0626.

40. 2016 Survey of America's physicians: practice patterns and perspectives. The Physician's Foundation. https://physiciansfoundation.org/wp-content/uploads/2017/12/ Biennial_Physician_Survey_2016.pdf

41. Shanafelt TD, Hasan O, Dyrbye LN, et al. Changes in burnout and satisfaction with work-life balance in physicians and the general US working population between 2011 and 2014. *Mayo Clin Proc*. 2015;90:1600-1613.

CPSIA information can be obtained
at www.ICGtesting.com
Printed in the USA
BVHW071220040720
582850BV00007B/12

9 780984 831074